SUNDAY'S CHILD
Times Past in Postcode DA11

Jean Hendy-Harris

Copyright 2019

Jean Hendy-Harris

Other books by this author

Chalk Pits and Cherry Stones

Eight Ten to Charing Cross

In Disgrace with Fortune

Memoirs, wartime, childhood in Kent, 1950s England

CONTENTS

1. The Demise of Kentish
2. Northfleet Village Green
3. The Difficult Business of Making Friends
4. A Case of The Dropsy On May Day
5. The Tenants of Tooley Street
6. Shepherd St Shenanigans
7. Buckingham Road & Blasts From The Past
8. Speaking of Springhead Road
9. Aunt Elsie
10. Troke's Shop
11. The Cobbler of Shepherd Street
12. A Career In The Movies
13. Huggens' College
14. A Decent Friendship at Wombwell Hall
15. The Two Miss Smiths
16. Old Gravesend Hospital in Bath Street
17. Wash Day
18. Brian Philpott
19. The Passing of Greta Thilthorpe
20. Local Pubs & Links with History
21. Of Cleaning & Cats
22. A Box at the Empire
23. The School Blazer
24. Homes For The Worthy Poor
25. Words & Music
26. A Remarkable Lack of Resilience
27. The Shipping Forecast
28. Broadcasting Carried On
29. In Sickness & In Health
30. The Coming of the Postcodes

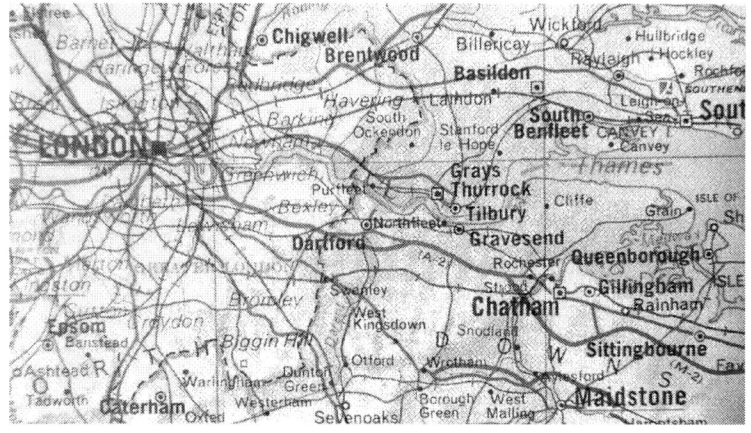

Northfleet in the centre of the map

The Demise of Kentish

Growing up in the outer reaches of Thameside Gravesend in the 1940s involved speaking a great deal of Old Kentish without actually realising it. None of us travelled very much back then and even a trip to Maidstone market was an Event with a capital E and so the expressions heard daily in the shops, pubs and streets of Swanscombe, Greenhithe, Northfleet and Gravesend formed the language that all of us accepted as standard. If someone had tried to explain what was dialect and what was accent we would have been not only immediately confused but disbelieving because as far as we were concerned it was only outsiders who had accents and therefore were treated with suspicion; the visiting aunt from far-off Leicester and the priest from Southern Ireland, and in any event did it really matter that words were pronounced differently in different areas when we were certain that our way was the right way? Time had to pass and we had to take excursions out of our immediate area on a regular basis in order to understand that some words immediately recognised by those around us might be completely incomprehensible to others living further afield and that this was nothing to do with accent and everything to do with dialect which in itself was fast disappearing. This fact would have been most unlikely, however, to disturb us in any way whatsoever.

In time our part of North Kent became disputed ground linguistically, a crossover area where local accent and dialect expressions became entangled and finally completely ensnared within the speech patterns of East and South London. Even as far back as when local master storyteller Charles Dickens was feverishly recording events of his imagination, the letter H was almost always silent and words beginning with W and V were variously interchangeable within this etymological no-man's land. Dickens himself would have doubtless been aware that at some stage the Kentish dialect had firmly divided itself into areas such as that primarily familiar to the East of the county and that more understood in the West. This was inevitable following the initiation of compulsory schooling in 1880 when the ideal for every child was to receive an education based on standard English and those venturing into teaching aspired to Speak Well and thus provide sound and sensible communication examples.

My maternal Grandmother Margaret Riorden, or Rearden depending on who was doing the spelling, was born around the time of The Act in Bethnal Green but somehow or other managed never to become involved with compulsory schooling. She always moved within a narrow circle of family, neighbours and itinerant agricultural workers and remained totally illiterate throughout her life, a fact that she considered had never held her back. She was certainly never in danger of having her vocal idioms contaminated by the example of enthusiastic schoolteachers or by the reading of either novels or newspapers. Until her death in 1965 her speech patterns remained firmly adhered to their origins first in Bethnal Green and later in North Kent where the family migrated when she was a small child. Along with the rest of her numerous grandchildren I came under her sphere of linguistic influence during my earliest years as we moved around daily from farm to farm for the harvesting of peas, beans, potatoes, stone fruit and hops depending upon the season.

Despite her lack of formal education or perhaps because of it, Old Nan developed an alarmingly strong personality and liked her presence to be felt. She could never have been described as a shrinking violet and let one and all know her opinions whether they made her popular or not. She was also a woman who was able to make quick decisions and influence those closest to her. Little wonder that her large family became heirs to her tongue and communication.

If she wanted to show approval for something she described herself as being *partial* to it, if we were unwell she said we were *peaky* and should we be cheeky to her, which we rarely were, we were *giving old lip*. She was glad to *see the back of* those she disliked and often described them as *giving her the pip*. Our heads were our *noddles* and the word *old* did not in itself necessarily refer to age but was an intensive expression when one of us *started a tidy old argument* or made a *tidy old sum* digging for potatoes in the space of a day. She would not of course lightly accept being *put upon* and a *right old paddy* might be the result. Places or people she took a dislike to became *one-eyed* and something out of alignment was *out of kilter*. If she rose late it was because she *overlaid* and there were times when her hip *gave her gip*.

These expressions passed effortlessly into the next generation so that each of my aunts would momentarily hesitate before wearing a red hat because they all were aware of *red hat, no drawers* and every one of my cousins knew what *feignights* meant in chasing games. It was my older cousin Margaret who taught us rhyme games such as the complicated finger rhyme, *Here's the church and here's the steeple, Open the doors and there's the people* and warned that you should carefully count the magpies noticed in a ploughed field before launching into, *One for sorrow, two for joy, three for a girl and four for a boy*. It was also Margaret who familiarised me on every trip on the 480 bus from Crayford to Northfleet with *Dirty Dartford, dirty people, bury their dead above the steeple* as we lumbered through that town.

We did not unduly concern ourselves with the weather as children but our mothers certainly understood what a *bitter-cold* day and a *black-dark* night were and that a brief shower was merely a *piddle*. In the early 1940s as we picked our way through the difficulties of the Second World War, we pre-schoolers absorbed it all and used it all along with the slightly nasal sing-song intonation that sat alongside it and was embodied in the very marshland and riverside environs in which we lived. Years later it was often this distinctive vocal timbre that would suddenly alert me to the presence of someone who hailed from North Kent being unmistakably the sound of my childhood.

Much of this Kentish language, though it was all around us, was fast becoming in danger of being abandoned with the advent of both radio and the Second World War. The war prompted us all to listen to radio broadcasts with greater attention than we might otherwise have done. My mother paid particular attention and I was persuaded to be as quiet as a mouse whilst she did so. Consequently I developed a fascination with the sounds made by those who read the news long before I was old enough for the speech patterns I had inherited from my antecedents to be diluted by the influence of school. I even determined that BBC English should be My English and did my best to emulate it which startled those around me until I learned that possibly it was not the best linguistic version for everyday use.

The end of the war brought street parties and less food rationing and heralded the next destructive push towards the demise of Kentish. The comparative ease of travel coincided with the television sets that slowly but determinedly crept into each working class home combining to enthusiastically destroy the paradigms of a local language that had until then changed little over two centuries. Our grandparents and great grandparents rarely ventured far from the immediate area into which they were born and although the delights of Hollywood were certainly available to my mother's generation, the language used by the American film industry was sufficiently removed from that spoken locally for it to barely cause a ripple among the firmly rooted expressions in use for generations. And even I, for all my upwardly mobile intent, was sensible enough to discard the speech idioms of Doris Day and Debbie Reynolds in favour of the disembodied vocal patterns of those who worked for the BBC.

So inevitably a large part of Kentish dialect is now out of reach to us in the twenty first century vanishing in the space of thirty or forty years. The passing has been so rapid that it would now be astonishing to hear on the streets of Gravesend or Northfleet an awkward person being described as *cack-handed* or a housewife forced into *dabbing out* on a wet Monday. The unwell are unlikely to feel *dicky* and the smartly dressed are no longer *all dogged up*. It would be a very elderly gentleman these days whose leg was *gammy*. If you feel doubtful or curious you are no longer *leery* and if you are tempted to steal fruit from orchards you probably wouldn't necessarily recognise that you were *scrumping*. We lose a language without noticing it and that which was an essential tool for human expression a few decades ago is suddenly gone.

Northfleet Village Green

Long before I was old enough to attend St Botolph's school in 1945, I was more than familiar with The Hill even if I didn't quite realise that it was regarded as the historical centre of old Northfleet. Once I did start school we were told that there had been a Church on The Hill as far back as Saxon times although nobody told us when exactly Saxon times were though I decided they had more than likely been even before my own grandmother was born. I had to get a great deal older before I realised that originally the area around the Church would have fallen gently towards the Thames on one side and the Ebbsfleet on the other and that strangely enough it had therefore not always been stranded on a narrow summit of land as it still is now. Nobody sees fit to explain how industry shapes landscape to children and so I grew up for the most part thinking that The Hill I knew had always been cut off precariously with cavernous drops on every side because of the excavation of chalk. Even when my grandmother spoke from time to time of the green fields present in her own grandmother's time I chose to doubt her because I preferred things to have always been the way I now knew them to be.

Old Minnie who lived in one of the now long gone cottages on The Hill and whose full name we never knew was once heard in conversation with Mr Will Clarke who had come to the school to teach us in about 1947, telling him the history of the place. He had been a Japanese POW and therefore was the kind of man who would be interested. She maintained that until the 1830s there was a pound and stocks where the Catholic Church then stood and still does although it was hard to imagine there had been a time when the Church was not in evidence. The pound was a small building made of the new-fangled bricks with a tiled roof and the stocks were somewhat closer to The Leather Bottel pub which was where the Parish Beadle had doled out suitable punishments to those who deserved them. Old Minnie said that foul-mouthed women were often put in the stocks and passers-by threw unmentionable objects at them. My friend Molly was certain that although people were said to throw eggs at those they disapproved of, that definitely wouldn't be true because eggs were too expensive. We decided it was probably stones although Siddy Ribbens suggested dog turds. Well he actually said dog shit but I was never allowed to use words like that even though my grandmother was prone to do so. I wondered if she would have been considered foul-mouthed enough to qualify for the stocks but didn't like to ask anybody's opinion. We learned that you also headed for the stocks if you misbehaved in Church although none of us could imagine what that might entail. Giving trouble in the Workhouse also might see you end up there if you weren't careful and although all of us were familiar with the term Workhouse because most of us had relatives who had at one time been inmates we knew it was nothing to be proud of and therefore should not be discussed. None of us in Mr Clarke's class were sure if the Workhouse was still in existence because when it was spoken of it was generally in terms that indicated a thankfulness that things had improved for society. It was David Reynolds whose father had something important to do with Northfleet

Station who finally asked the question and Mr Clarke told us that the Workhouse in nearby Gravesend had been closed for almost fifty years and was now St James's Hospital. However, at one time Northfleet had boasted its very own Workhouse nearby at Granby Place, and probably built in about 1700. Originally the building had been a boarding school but by 1820 it had become the Northfleet Workhouse which it remained for about twenty years. The place had disappeared completely by the late 1880s and the grounds had then become part of the churchyard.

Mr Clarke was the kind of teacher you don't easily forget if you are interested in odd bits and pieces of social history which I was. He told us that in 1860 a tollgate was erected adjacent to the Leather Bottel and this had come about because of the railway. David Reynolds nodded and we felt that his family was more important than ever and somehow part of it all. A group of people called The Turnpike Commissioners, after a great deal of debate and argument, decided that this extra tollgate was urgently needed because so much money was being lost due to the advent of the railway. Apparently the decision was not popular with local shopkeepers as they were forced to pay a toll each time they ventured onto Dover, London or Springhead Roads. Nevertheless it lasted for ten years until the office of the Turnpike Commissioners was itself disbanded in 1871. Fashion-conscious local women heaved sighs of relief because even those who could easily afford the toll were more than annoyed by the fact that the gate was too narrow to easily accommodate their crinoline skirts.

These days the Roman Catholic Church stands out as a prominent if rather stark feature on the local landscape and has done so since it was erected in 1914. Apparently a local benefactor, Mr Alfred Tolhurst, provided the funds needed – the sizeable sum of eight thousand pounds and of course had his own pew inside. Once my father returned from the war I was to visit regularly for Sunday mass but I always saw it as a grim and gloomy place and much preferred the welcoming warmth of Anglican St. Botolph's. Sometimes my friend Molly and I went into the gloomy interior of the place simply to dare each other to touch the cold and dark statues without exhibiting fear. Once, accompanied by Kathleen McCarthy, we were astonished to see her do so without a qualm and decided that being possessed of red hair was an advantage where courage was concerned. It had certainly advantaged Queen Boadicia of whom we had learned relatively recently and been told that as Kentish women we should be proud of her and call her Boudicca. All of this information had come from Mr Clarke of course.

To the right of this forbidding religious structure was Penny, Son and Parker's grocery, a place frequented by us all on a regular basis. This was where we queued patiently at least twice weekly to buy sugar to be weighed out into cones and broken biscuits and bacon. On one momentous occasion Molly and I, dancing together along Springhead Road, she as Doris Day and me as Ginger Rogers, found that the one pound note that had been at the bottom of the shopping basket when we set out had now disappeared. In total panic we searched each side of Springhead Road twice before returning to

31 York Road in terror to report the loss to her mother. And her long suffering mother with a shake of her head and a tear in her eye searched her purse and along the mantelpiece for replacement coins and crossed several items from the list but Molly was not beaten as I might have been. My own mother was clearly of a more punitive bent as far as her children were concerned. We returned to Penny, Son and Parker's in a more sober fashion, Molly clutching the coins in her right hand. It was shortly after this episode that the shop that had been serving the public for five decades, closed its doors for ever and we wondered if we had somehow brought bad luck to the place.

Once there had been old weatherboard cottages at 5 and 6 The Hill but they were said to have been demolished in the middle of the nineteenth century and replaced by two purpose-built brick shops, one of which was a newsagents. My mother said that she remembered it being a Fancy Bazaar years before but I had no idea what a Fancy Bazaar might be. In the late 1940s as well as newspapers and comics you could buy sherbert dabs and liquorice wood and acid drops in this particular establishment and Cut-Out Paper Doll Books which were expensive at one and sixpence each but which I longed to own. Mrs Bassant, our neighbour, told me that years ago you didn't need to buy your daily newspaper if you took The Times because you could borrow it for a penny and take it back when you'd finished reading it. When I asked her how long you could have the loan of it for she didn't know but I thought it a very odd arrangement and wondered what would happen if you accidentally tore a page or didn't return it for a week.

On the south east corner of the area that was once the Village Green and is now a car park, was a butcher's shop that had been there for more than a hundred years and boasted its own slaughter house. The first owner did a great deal of upgrading and made improvements in 1790 and replaced the old-fashioned weather boarding with smart new bricks. Old Minnie told a terrifying story that involved the slaughter house harbouring a number of murdered bodies but added comfortingly that in the end the story turned out not to have been true. Nevertheless Molly and I still shivered theatrically whenever we passed the place, especially as the old hooks and rails for hanging carcasses were still in evidence. These days it is a pharmacy and the last time I was there I could not help but notice that the legendary hooks still remain.

There were a number of cottages facing The Green on the south side and Mr Clarke said that one Billy Skews, a veteran of the Battle of Waterloo, had lived at No 10. He had lost an arm in the battle and for many years had a stall in Gravesend Market selling confectionery which he and his wife made themselves. He also sold his wares at the Easter Fair held on The Hill each year. When I was a child, however, No 10 was an undertaker's and apparently still is. There had been more than one annual fair in the old days and originally they were so busy they had been held in nearby fields big enough to accommodate the many amusements and sideshows. The busiest fair was usually that held on St Botolph's day in mid-June and attracted visitors from far and wide. By the time Billy Skews was selling his confectionery the fairs were already losing their appeal. This was something else to be blamed on the Railway, transporting people as it did so effortlessly to the delights of places further afield like Southend and Margate. And there of course in the fullness of time were the more technically advanced attractions of Dodgem Cars and Ferris Wheels courtesy of Dreamworld and The Kursaal. You could quite understand why the families of Kent were no longer as enthralled with the idea of home-made confectionery and bearded ladies. Personally, however, I was not particularly fond of the more up to the minute seaside funfairs and nursed a deep fear and suspicion of the technology involved in lifting paying customers far from the ground and flinging them around in garishly decorated pseudo-vehicles. I would have infinitely preferred a decorous saunter through a field of Two Headed Babies and Three Armed Men. This preference was not something I shared with my peers as I had no desire to be jeered at or bullied by neighbourhood children and classmates. Anyone currently between the ages of five and fourteen will tell you how preferable it is to hold the same likes, dislikes and desires as those around you.

    On the opposite side of The Green there was once an Inn called The Dove, apparently one of the most ancient in Northfleet but it had burned down in 1906. Behind the Inn was a huddle of old cottages in Dove Yard that were still standing in the 1940s. Just to the right, The Coach and Horses, dating from 1572 still stands and I have a memory or two of under-age drinking involving gin and tonic there as a teenager. Adjoining it were a number of 17th century cottages that were apparently demolished in the late 1950s. I should remember this because I would undoubtedly have viewed it as vandalism, but sadly I don't. In one of them lived a woman most of us had decided was a witch when we were still young enough to readily believe in witches. Recently I learned she was actually the mother of Ron Hull, local poet who wrote so eloquently of the area and whose slim volumes of poetry are now so difficult to find. Directly behind the pub was the site of Northfleet's very first purpose-built fire station. Originally it was a Volunteer Service but at the beginning of the second world war had become fully incorporated into the National Fire Service.

On the final side of the triangle that formed The Green, The Queen's Head pub stood and was run when I was a child by the McCarthys, parents of the red haired Kathleen and said to be well off. Kathleen's mother bought her black ballet style shoes and let her have her hair permed and her ears pierced so of course we envied her and she knew it and was prone to showing off. The pub had previously been called The Crown and at that time had extensive grounds to the rear of the building including a bowling green. After a disastrous fire in 1830 the building had to be renovated completely and the bowling green somehow or other disappeared along with the ever more urgent quest for chalk. The Post Office stood adjacent to the pub and there was still a sub post office there when I was a teenager. I remember that the woman who worked there sat behind a grille and had a fascinating hole in her neck which blinked repetitively. My mother told me she had to breathe through the hole because of an operation on her throat and that it was rude to stare. I couldn't help staring, however, and the unfortunate woman fascinated me so much I was both fearful and delighted to be sent in to buy postage stamps.

Maureen Barlow who was in our class when we were ten and wanted to be a nurse said that the device in the woman's throat was called a Stoma and when you had one you could no longer speak properly. I had not even noticed that the woman behind the grille no longer spoke properly.

Next door to the Post Office there had once been a grocery store where you could buy real coffee beans but when I was growing up and familiar only with Camp Coffee Essence, it had become a second-hand book shop, run largely I believe as a hobby as it only seemed to open sporadically. There all kinds of fascinating volumes could be bought for mere pence and it was due to its existence that I began to build up my own albeit small library in 1950 starting with an unlikely story called *The Girl Crusoes* concerning three schoolgirls marooned on a Pacific Island and forced to live on all manner of exotic fruits and vegetables including Breadfruit and Yams. I remember little else about the story.

At the turn of the 20th century The Green was at last paved over for some reason and in time a First World War Memorial was erected from Portland Stone to commemorate those local servicemen who lost their lives during the conflict. Today the monument has become hemmed in on every side by vehicles that nudge each other for space and the area has changed completely. St Botolph's School disappeared some years ago and on my last visit a temporary garden centre had situated itself in what had been the Infants' Playground . The Church lych gate still stands defiantly, harbouring the memory of those mothers of the 1940s who sheltered there on rainy afternoons whilst waiting to collect their five and six year-olds from the clutches of Miss Honour who was young and pretty with long blonde hair and Mrs Johnson who was short and dumpy and rather fierce and always wore a flowered smock to protect her twin set.

I am reliably informed that there is now a new St Botolph's School nearby but as yet I have not investigated it, so wedded am I to the idea that there can really only be one – the one I attended for six years, on The Hill, or as Ron Hull more accurately describes it - Northfleet Village Green.

The Difficult Business of Making Friends

By the time I started school in September 1945 the war was firmly over, even the conflict in the Pacific that we in Northfleet knew little of and so were not much concerned with. We had long had our street parties in every corner of the county and were even bored with the idea of wearing our red, white and blue hair ribbons. Fathers had begun to return home in June, sporting smart new demob suits and shiny shoes and within a short space of time stopped spoiling their offspring with days out to Southend-on-Sea and games of football and started making demands on them to sit up straight when they were eating and make better efforts to be helpful to their mothers. My own father, because of an illness he had contracted in the North African desert, did not make an appearance in person until October and so to me remained a photograph on the wall that had to be blown kisses on my way to bed. I started school therefore with the full attention of my mother who was confident that now a whole new range of possibilities was open to me and I would quickly make friends and become a popular and successful student in next to no time! It was abundantly clear that having experienced a somewhat chequered school career herself, she wanted better for me. Her own problems with school had mirrored those of her sisters – they simply did not attend often enough for it to be of much benefit to them. This was because they were so frequently needed to take part in seasonal field work and also to care for younger siblings.

Some people seem to find themselves in the happy position of going through life making friends extremely easily and rising to the top in the popularity stakes of each group they become involved with. I'm definitely not one of them and I have always envied those who were. I have had few really close friends over the years and fewer still when I was a child. Molly from No 31 York Road was something of an exception in that she remained my friend over a number of years and did not particularly criticise me or demand very much of me; perhaps she simply did not like me as much as I liked her but possibly a further clue lies in the fact that I never selected her as a suitable victim for my most manipulative schemes. My mother, clearly disappointed in me, always maintained that my unpopularity lay in the fact that I was a very Quarrelsome Child. She spoke with a fair degree of accuracy although Quarrelsome was not a word I would have immediately chosen. However my general behaviour dictated that it was not completely unsurprising that I found it difficult to make and maintain close childhood relationships. Even at the time I knew there was a problem and half realised why but seemed unable to make the necessary changes for the better. I told myself that it didn't matter because I didn't really care – but of course I did.

 It began whilst I was still a pre-schooler when Evelyn the granddaughter of The Bassants Next Door would have become my friend very willingly had I only treated her a little better. But treating her well seemed unmanageable and whilst on the surface I appeared to be her friend, behind the scenes and out of the way of adult eyes I made her life as miserable as any four year old possibly could. I plagued her with taunts regarding her weight, jeered at the stories she told me about her mother swallowing open safety pins on a regular basis (that miraculously closed when they encountered mysteriously placed bones whilst navigating her digestive tract) and perhaps more spitefully, sent her on treasure hunts that forced her to purloin other people's possessions. Even this thinly disguised theft might not have been so bad had Evelyn been allowed to keep at least some of the plunder for herself but generally I required her to hand it over. One day she found a full sized cricket bat that had clearly been mistakenly left on The Old Green and she rushed with great excitement to tell me about it. We should play cricket together she told me, still glowing with the exhilaration of the find. Not wanting to admit that I had not a clue as to how cricket was played, however, I decided to spoil things for her by claiming loudly to her grandparents that in fact the bat had been found by me and Evelyn had stolen it from me and I wanted it back. The grandparents looked doubtful but within minutes I was sobbing convincingly great victim sobs and so it was handed over. I've often wondered why I felt the need to do that as had no inclination to play sport and the bat was shoved under my bed and destined never to be used again.

I saved my most socially hostile schemes for my years at St Botolph's School so that other, more amiable classmates, once they got the measure of me generally did their best not to get too close and in any activity where we had to Choose a Partner, I was invariably left un-partnered and for ever destined to work alongside whoever happened to be the other class misfit at the time. In Miss Biggs' class at the age of eight I found myself sitting next to another York Road resident, Peter

Jackson, a fairly inoffensive boy as boys go who made it clear he would have much rather been placed beside another boy – any boy. For several weeks I made his life miserable by regularly writing the rudest words I knew in his exercise books in capital letters. By today's standards the words were reasonably mundane and I remember SHIT, BUM, TITS and BUGGER but nothing more indecent than that. However Peter was outraged and when he importantly strode to the front of the room, exercise book in hand, to advise Miss Biggs of this ignominy I practised looking as guileless as possible and with a confused little shrug told her that I didn't know why Peter said such things about me and I only wished he would stop writing rude words. I even contemplated asking her what TITS actually meant before deciding against the idea. She always believed me and invariably Peter would be told he had to stay in at playtime as a punishment – or given a hundred lines to remind himself that writing rude words was totally unacceptable. I finally stopped torturing him in this manner when he was one day sent to Mr Cook the new headmaster who caned him. Even I thought that was excessive and I found myself so strangely moved by his tears that I began to cry myself. Miss Biggs advised both of us to stop crying at once and reminded me that Peter had been a very naughty boy indeed – that I was the real victim and I should on no account feel sorry for him!

Back in the late 1940s Britain was just beginning to recover from the effects of the war, fathers mostly had regular jobs and even working class children like the majority of St Botolph's pupils were given regular small amounts of pocket money. Although saving was encouraged by most adults the recipients of the money were infinitely keener on spending it on such delicacies as liquorice wood, sherbet dabs and locust beans from the newsagent and sweet shop next to Penney Son & Parkers on The Hill. To say I was envious of the beneficiaries of these weekly sums is an understatement and I discussed it at some length with Molly who was another non-receiver. Finally I hit upon the idea of collecting from what I saw as the more affluent homes in Springhead Road for a non-existent charity which I called the NSSSC (National Society for the Salvation of School Children). Molly wisely declined to join me in this venture but eventually I persuaded a nicely behaved girl called Betty Haddon from Hartfield Place who said she was keen but only if the eventual collection really and truly benefited school children. I told her we were going to buy sherbet dabs and I would personally post them to children in Africa who needed saving.

Although Betty had been reasonably easily convinced, the scheme was not as successful as I had hoped and we were asked rather a lot of penetrating questions about how long we had been Registered but eventually we collected two shillings and nine pence which bought quite a number of sherbet dabs I seem to remember. I generously tried to give Betty one to take home with her but she said she didn't want it because her Mum would ask her questions about it. I was bemused by this attitude and because I had never been totally wedded to the idea of posting such delightful goodies to Africa in the first place, I consumed the remainder myself over the next day or two. Sadly, when I approached Betty for a second round of after school collecting she firmly refused and at playtime went back to playing skipping with Barbara Scutts and Rita Jenkins. When I tried to join them Barbara, who was bossy as well as popular, said they had enough for their game and I was not allowed to play. Feeling wounded I told Barbara she had stinky knickers whereupon she said that my mother dressed me funny. Because that might possibly be true given my mother's poor dressmaking skills I ran away at that point and seethed in the girls' toilets planning suitable payback. Walking home from school Molly said she had never thought Collecting for the NSSSC was a very good idea in the first place.

 A year or so later I briefly became friendly with Helen Gunner the local vicar's daughter. I was in fact quite gratified to have been able to coerce her into friendship because she had an attractively verging on Posh voice and at that stage I was still trying to perfect my BBC accent and it was clear she was in a position to help being very nearly Posh herself. It was also clear that though they tried to push the rather un-Christian impression aside, her parents considered me to be a totally unsuitable friend for their daughter. Their gut feeling hardened when I encouraged her to play Noughts & Crosses for money and she ended up owing me nearly seven shillings. We had started off with very minor farthing stakes but after a while, to increase the excitement of the game I suggested we progress to Double or Nothing and by that time I think I had also somehow or other rigged the outcome. The Reverend Gunner took us into his rather impressively book-lined study and gave us a gentle lecture on the evils of gambling during which I began to cry and told him that part of me knew it wasn't right but I was saving up to buy my mother a brooch for her birthday. Helen began to cry as well at that stage and pointed out in a more than slightly moralistic and uptight manner that I had, after all, won the money fairly and squarely and it wasn't really my fault that gambling was so unacceptable. She even ventured with some hesitation that it was possible no-one had ever explained that properly to me before. Her father began to falter and I saw him wavering, wanting to support his daughter's sense of what was Fair, Moral, Just – more than a little bit proud of her. In fact exactly like a father in a story book! I thought it must be reassuring to have parents like him although I could see the downside also – just imagine being constantly reminded about the rights and wrongs of your behaviour. At least bottom of the heap families like mine rarely went in for lectures on moral behaviour and most reprimands and punishment simply revolved around drawing attention to yourself by annoying an adult when it wasn't strictly necessary to do so. Whilst I was meditating upon these differences between families, to my amazement Reverend Gunner handed over the seven shillings and said there would be no further debate on the matter. I did notice, however, that the following Monday at school Helen avoided me and had soon found a new Best Friend – Elizabeth. Feeling more than a little irked I asked her why and she justified the shift by telling me that Elizabeth went to the same tap dancing class as she did. How I envied those fortunate few who were allowed to attend dance classes and set off importantly each Wednesday after school clutching shoe bags made by loving mothers containing tap shoes.

By the time I was ten I had become more pragmatic about the difficult business of attracting friends. It was just possible I was a Late Developer as far as friends were concerned like my cousin Desmond who had caused a great deal of family gossip because he didn't say a single word until he was three. Even Old Nan agreed that he was finally as Right as Rain and some children simply developed late. Friendship might be something I would eventually grow into.

A Case of The Dropsy on May Day

During my first years of school the headmaster at St Botolph's was Mr Tilley and I have no memory of him whatsoever. Once I recovered from the initial trauma of those very first few school days, the feeling of being abandoned, the loss of my mother's full time attention, I quite enjoyed school, finding the teachers, the buildings, playgrounds, the church and most especially the tranquil nearby churchyard a welcome change from the confines of York Road where the downside of my mother's devotion was that her word was Law. School offered a range of other adults who had power and influence that I soon realised in many ways superseded my mother's. She had a love-hate relationship with both School and Church, had been treated badly by the zealous Crayford Sisters of Mercy because of constant absenteeism and it was undoubtedly these memories that led to me being enrolled in an Anglican school. This was an act that was to greatly perturb my decidedly more devout father once he reappeared into our lives around the middle of that first school term.

I recall the school staff with a certain amount of affection – Miss Honour, Mrs Johnson, Mrs Allen and Miss Biggs, all of whom were sound teachers and basically kind. All were eclipsed, however, by Mr Clarke whose teaching was at times inspirational and whose pupils without exception loved him dearly. The boys were particularly intrigued that he had been a fighter pilot during the war and was shot down and became a POW. This information did not emotionally move the girls nearly as much of course but Will Clarke was able to enthuse and motivate each one of us in a way that eludes many teachers.

It was during my second year with Mr Clarke that I first became aware of the headmaster who had replaced Mr Tilley, the tyrannical Mr Cook who, towards the end of that year and quite out of the blue began to teach us Arithmetic on Friday afternoons. Academically I was in no way outstanding, although this was a fact my ever hopeful father found difficult to process, and Arithmetic was definitely my weakest subject. For me it had been bad enough trying to master fractions and long division under the kindly guidance of Mr Clarke but became all but impossible beneath the direction of the terrifying Mr Cook. Friday afternoons had formerly been a serene and peaceful time devoted to ideas and to books. Mr Clarke discussed with us all manner of interesting ideas such as the rights and wrongs of cannibalism and what human flesh might taste like. John Dyke wanted to know if he meant when it was raw or when it was cooked and Mr Clarke paused momentarily before assuring him that he meant when it was cooked. Wendy Maxted who rarely said much raised her head at once and wanted to know exactly how it would have been cooked. A few of the other girls began to titter nervously but Mr Clarke treated that question seriously also and explained that he thought it might have been simmered in a cauldron with roots and vegetables and perhaps a few herbs. This cooking method and the resulting taste was then hotly debated until Mr Clarke told us that he had heard that human flesh when cooked with care tasted a little bit like lamb. With that we were silenced although I found myself contemplating this interesting morsel of information on every future occasion when the Sunday roast featured lamb.

Mr Clarke led us into a discussion as to whether or not children would ever be allowed to vote and if so what political path we might each pursue, listening to the reasons why our families were Labour or Conservative without passing comment. A substantial number of us surprisingly perhaps supported the Conservatives and one boy admitted to having a father who was Communist and fervently supported Collective Farming. The rest of us did not understand how that particular form of agriculture worked and Mr Clarke enthusiastically explained. Those of us who lost interest and became bored by these Friday afternoon debates were allowed to doodle or fall asleep without comment. It was also a time when we were introduced to poetry – *The Lady of Shalott, Daffodils, The Destruction of Sennacherib* and were urged to expand our reading to *The Snow Goose* and the *Myths of Ancient Greece and Rome*. For these reasons I have never been able to forget Mr Clarke. Six decades later Molly Freeman, now determinedly beginning to master the use of email, sent me an excited message because she had by an odd accident of fate involving an article about football in a local paper, rediscovered Will Clarke, then in his nineties and living in The Midlands. We were ecstatic to make contact once again with the man who had deftly turned what might have been completely ordinary primary school years into a time during which learning became distinctive and exceptional. And Mr Clarke, more than at ease with the intricacies of electronic messaging, communicated with each of us vigorously and deliberated all aspects of those

St Botolph's days. We learned that his time at the school had not always been as uncomplicated as our own and that the loss of his teenage son in a road accident had all but paralysed him emotionally. We also began to understand that the demands placed upon him and the rest of the school staff by the most unpopular headmaster, Mr Cook, had made life anything but enjoyable and had caused him to examine the reasons why he stayed more than once. You could say that Mr Cook wreaked just as much misery upon the staff as he did upon the students.

I have never forgotten this man's alarming lessons although fortunately for we girls it was the boys who were the main focus of his sadism. Most of the time we were left to be horrified observers as he pulled students from behind desks by their ears, closed desk lids onto fingers with his feet, shook them until their teeth rattled, all the time screaming at the front row unfortunates, his face turning puce and the veins in his neck bulging. Largely these brutal episodes were instigated simply by an unlucky ten-year-old failing to understand some aspect of multiplication. Simply witnessing these Friday afternoon rages firmed up my dislike of Mathematics in all its forms and turned it into a fully-fledged phobia. My York Road neighbour, Pearl Banfield, was so terrified that on two occasions she fainted at the beginning of the class and was able to rest on a bench in the cloakroom for the duration. Henceforth her mother invariably collected her on Friday lunchtimes and she simply disappeared for the afternoon. I thought this was a splendid idea but my own mother was not as kindly and understanding and simply advised I should just keep my head down.

Mr Cook had clearly arrived at St Botolph's intending to Make a Difference. This turned out not to be merely limited to mathematical outcomes which in retrospect I realised had something to do with the eleven plus examination we were to take the following year, but spread into other areas also. One of his initial ideas was to reintroduce the peculiar festival of the Boy Bishop whose fate was somehow associated with the Feast of Fools. His explanations of this custom did little to help us understand it. We were warned, however, that it was our duty to remember what he was telling us so that we would be able to deliver every detail to our parents and impress upon them how important the festival was. It seemed to revolve around selecting a boy from the choir early in December to play the part of the Bishop on St Nicholas' Day somehow parodying the real Bishop, the game proceeding until the Christmas pageant. However, to our enormous relief the whole idea was abandoned after one trial because of a marked lack of interest from anyone in the community. The greatest relief was expressed by the Boy Bishop himself who was horrified to find that he was expected to write his own weekly sermons for the duration.

He then launched Saturday Evening Socials for Families. Parents and grandparents were expected to attend and possibly even well behaved, older children. Younger children were most definitely not welcome but my mother had found this ruling hard to internalise. The Socials took place on a monthly basis and the entire staff was present, Mr Clarke having the job of amusing those children who were forced to accompany their parents. As I was one of them on several occasions along with my little brother, I saw this as a splendid idea although I remember feeling distinctly nervous about the possible behaviour of my pre-school sibling. The huge and rumbling partition in the Infants' Department was rolled back for these occasions and parents were served cups of tea and sponge cake that Mrs. Johnson and Mrs Allen had been ordered to make for the event. Despite the best efforts of all the adults the gatherings were glacial affairs where those families gutsy enough to attend showed deference to Mr Cook and complimented him on the Huge Difference he was making to the children's learning. He in his turn, wearing a smart tweed jacket with leather patches on the elbows, smiled big smiles that did not quite reach his eyes and drummed the fingers of his left hand on the top of tables laden with cups and saucers and cake.

I found the unfamiliar intimacy between home and school both exciting and chilling and more than conducive to taking wild chances. I used the final occasion on which my parents attended to steal a poetry book from our classroom bookshelf, stuffing it down my knickers and spending the rest of the evening and the walk home in great discomfort. I then worried for weeks that it might have been missed but was at the same time ecstatic to have become the owner of *A Child's Garden of Verses*.

Of course there were miscreant parents who failed to make an appearance at any one of these awkward and uneasy events but those foolhardy enough to attend once were expected to continue to do so and future failure meant that their offspring were cross examined at Monday morning assemblies as to the reasons why. When I finally found myself being interrogated I was sick with fear and gave various explanations ranging from my father being on the night shift, which might have been true to my mother falling down stairs and breaking both her knees, which definitely was not.

Another one of Mr Cook's brilliant ideas was the celebration of May Day with traditional Maypole dancing and the making of May Dolls. We were informed of this at the conclusion of one of the disturbing Maths classes whilst Billy Elliot, having drawn attention to himself by not knowing immediately what the required answer to One Fifth Of One Hundred was, nursed his injured fingers beneath his armpit and tried hard to stifle his tears. Mothers of the girls, we were told as the darkly snake-like eyes of the Headmaster examined each of our respectfully bent female heads, were to each make a May Doll by the end of the month. These dolls, it was further explained, were to be placed in shoe boxes and decorated with flowers which we might make ourselves out of tissue paper and pipe cleaners. Then, all being well with the arrangement of both dolls and flowers, we girls would be escorted in a group to visit local cottages and even houses of the gentry such as the Thames River Pilot and the Doctor who both lived not a stone's throw away in London Road, to show off our combined handiwork. We might even be rewarded with pennies which we would be allowed to keep.

Jacqueline Haskell, whose mother was a shorthand typist and occasionally helped out in the school office ventured to enquire in a very small voice indeed what a May Doll was actually for and wouldn't it be more time efficient if we simply utilised a normal doll such as we might already have at home in order to save our mothers a lot of unnecessary work. At least although she didn't put it quite that way, that was the gist of her query. The rest of us exchanged glances, astonished at her daring. Mr Cook's neck pulse throbbed several times before a short explanation was given but I was so absorbed in watching the throb of the pulse that the details escaped me. Impressed with Jacqueline's nerve I toyed with the idea of asking what we should do if we were a family without a spare shoe box. The only shoe boxes in our house were used for the storage of important documents such as old ration books and birth certificates and various family snapshots taken by my father with his Brownie camera. I did not quite have the necessary courage, however.

Instead I asked Pearl as I walked home with her. She was crying quietly and saying that her mother would not have time to make a May Doll by the end of the month let alone find a shoe box in which to put it. I comforted her with the fact that it was more likely than not that my mother would find herself in the same position. During that Spring of 1948 we each found ourselves giving our mothers what must have been tedious daily reminders presumably along with all the other girls. The May celebrations loomed over us like a huge sword of Damocles and I found myself having anxiety dreams about shoe boxes. Now, each afternoon, we were taken to the park by the station, to practice Maypole dancing under the direction of Mr Clarke with help from Mrs

Haskell and Billy Elliot's mother who was either keen to become involved or intent upon protecting her son from further assault should Mr Cook himself decide to drop by to assess progress. We were told that for the event itself we would wear brightly coloured sashes which was a relief because when the idea was first mooted there had been a suggestion that white dresses for the girls might be involved which the mothers would also have to make by the end of the month.

By the end of April, despite a great deal of negative advice from my grandmother that made me sick with terror because it included suggestions for Going Round That Bleeding School and Cleaning That Silly Bugger Headmaster Rotten, I had a May Doll made from an old sock with button eyes and yellow woollen plaited hair suitably surrounded by pink crepe paper flowers made by my cousin Margaret and nestling inside a shoe box that had previously contained her father's Christmas Day carpet slippers. Pearl's doll was beautiful, dressed in a skirt of parachute silk with a matching bonnet and so lovely it was carried to and from school on the back of her brother's bike. Only poor little Maureen Dunstan who had seven siblings and wore clothes that my mother said were Shameful, was without a doll and she cried in a corner whilst the rest of us looked disapprovingly in her direction. Jaqueline even asked whether she should be allowed to dance at the Maypole at all in her doll-less state.

We were reminded more than once that all mothers and grandparents were expected to attend the Maypole Dancing and what was more, that a photographer from The Gravesend Reporter would be coming to take a photograph that was to appear in the paper. The idea of having our photographs in the local paper was of course thrilling but for me also perturbing as my greatest area of shame was being possessed of the kind of grandmother who did not behave as grandmothers are supposed to behave. Old Nan had never been known to bake a birthday cake or in fact show the slightest bit of love and affection towards her grandchildren and, to add insult to injury, she was inclined to the most unacceptable and vulgar turn of phrase. I imagined a photograph of a possible stand-off between Old Nan and Mr Cook and the visions that flashed before me were alarming.

On 30th April Mr Cook demanded confirmation of all family members who would be attending the ceremony and most especially which Grandparents. There followed several seconds of absolute silence before Jennifer Berryman said that her grandmother was sorry, she would have loved to come but she was too ill with The Dropsy, a condition that sounded delightfully serious. Mr Cook's body twitched and he looked as if he would have liked to divest the planet of both Jennifer and her grandmother but he made no comment. Then Wendy Selves said her grandmother lived too far away in Margate and Peter Jackson said his grandmother was going into hospital and his grandfather had to look after the cats. Margaret Snelling said that she didn't actually have a grandmother which I knew to be a lie. Mr Cook still said nothing but his eyes slowly traversed the tops of our heads. Feeling more confident now I raised my own hand and said my grandmother was also too ill with The Dropsy and then to fill the silence I added that there was a lot of it about and she was almost dead with it in fact.

My heart pounded but the headmaster remained totally silent.

There were far fewer spectators than expected at the May Day Event which did not please Mr Cook at all but I was relieved and almost proud that my mother was present and wearing the new hat my father had given her at Christmastime. Pearl's mother was wearing a smart blue two-piece costume and a velvet hat shaped like a shell with a piece of net across the front. Both her grandmothers were there! My mother sniffed and said that was because the Banfields were Smarmy but she said it quietly and nobody else heard her. I knew that had she been present Old Nan would have said much worse and it was a very good thing she had such a bad case of The Dropsy. The photograph that went into the Saturday paper was excellent.

The Tenants of Tooley Street

Although I became comfortably familiar with our immediate York Road neighbours as a pre-schooler, I was blissfully unaware of those living in surrounding streets until I was considerably older.

The families from Tooley Street where there were a mere twenty-eight houses were even considered rather detached from us in York Road because of the Old Green that lay between us. It stretched out like a meadow in my mind, fertile and verdant, a grassy expanse giving life to an abundance of dandelions, buttercups and daisies valiantly fighting their way through the chalky subsoil. If I climbed onto our back gate as I frequently did, I could see just a few of the Tooley Street houses and they were places where groups of rough and frightening boys armed with catapults lived. One afternoon when still a pre-schooler I had persuaded my mother to let me out of the gate to pick wild flowers and was attacked by an alarming group of eight and nine year olds who told me that the Old Green was their territory and that I should Bugger Off. My first instinct was to retreat to the safety of our own yard as fast as possible but something forced me to stand my ground whilst trying desperately to think of a belligerent retort that would make them believe I was at least as tough and unafraid as someone who went to school. The only word that came out, however, was a strangled No. The boys withdrew to the outer edge of the Old Green and for a blissful moment I imagined I had won the first round of this particular confrontation. I turned back to gathering dandelions feeling just a little bit taller. Bystanders must surely think I was at least five years old and not just turned four. This joyous feeling lasted until the pebble from the catapult hit my upper thigh and the biggest boy shouted out to never, ever to talk back to him because his name was Daring Dexter and not to forget that. When my mother caught up with him as he fled however, it turned out that his name was not Daring Dexter at all but Siddy Ribbens and that he had not meant for the pebble to hit me. It had all been a mistake.

Apparently there had once been houses standing on the Old Green but that was well into the past. The Old Green had been there long before the war. It was there when my parents moved into 28 York Road in August 1939 but Old Mrs Bassant next door said that there had definitely been houses on it during the previous war. Whether that was so or not, the unexpected expanse of grassland made a splendid playground for local children even though we were constantly told to be wary of Dene Holes. Apparently falling into a Dene Hole was tantamount to falling to your death and had certainly claimed lives in the past. Not comprehending the dangers involved we largely ignored the warnings. Much of the bricks and mortar that had formed the original buildings still remained and were used and reused by at least two generations of children to become forts, mansions and department stores or simply to delineate play houses that emulated those we already lived in.

As time passed I became more familiar with the tenants of Tooley Street. No 17 on the corner was where George and Elsie Bull ran their corner shop. We didn't see much of George who spent most of his time in the back reading the racing papers and left the running of the business to Aunt Elsie, a small plump and bespectacled woman who sold newspapers, tobacco, ice cream and sweets, the latter from tall glass jars. Lemon Drops, Bulls Eyes, Aniseed Balls, Liquorice All Sorts, Toffees and much more, all of which could be purchased in one ounce lots by local children with restricted financial resources. Further up the street at 21 lived the Davis Family with Grandmother Edith the Davis matriarch. Alma and John had four attractive and always smartly turned out children: Ann, John, Hedley and Ellison. John Davis Senior had not served during the war because he was engaged in War Work and this fact, when applied to men of serving age, always brought out the worst in my mother who was tight-lipped and said that the Likes of Him didn't know how lucky they were. Later on John Davis Senior was not so fortunate when he dropped dead to the consternation of both customers and staff in the Dover Road pharmacy waiting for a prescription to be filled. He had just come from a consultation with the local doctor who had told him the pains in his chest were nothing to worry about.

But long before this could happen the two youngest Davis boys were born and each named after the junior doctor who had delivered him – Hedley and Ellison. This love affair Mrs Davis had with the medical profession not surprisingly ceased after the death of her husband. Ann, the oldest was the talk of Tooley Street and beyond when in her final school year she fell in love with a merchant seaman, causing her mother a great deal of anguish. So much so that she banned the relationship completely and would not even allow the young man's letters to be delivered. Ann, with admirable efficiency, merely organised for them to be sent instead to the Buckingham Road address of an elderly neighbour who said she knew how it felt to be young and in love. It was said that the object of her own affections had been gassed during the First World War. It was a solution to the problem that mesmerised those of us similar in age to Ann herself and scandalised the older generation who then as one gave the do-gooder The Cold Shoulder. Whether Mrs Davis ever found out about the arrangement is lost with the passage of time but Ann could be seen on Monday mornings in her school uniform on her bike, stopping outside the Buckingham Road house to enquire if any mail had arrived. Needless to say Molly and I were both enormously impressed by Ann's bold audacity and felt she was a model to us all. Ann went on to marry very early, possibly to the very same object of her affections, and become a teenage mother, again to the admiration and envy of many of her former classmates and neighbours and the tight lipped disapproval of our parents.

Mrs Maxted and her daughter Wendy lived at No 19 but I have no recollection if a Mr Maxted existed or indeed if Wendy had any siblings. She was a well behaved girl who wasn't usually allowed to have too much to do with the headstrong Ann Davis. Her hair was always in neat plaits and even at primary school she wore a gymslip and white blouse which I thought set her apart from the rest of us. Molly said she had inherited it from an older cousin, a Colyer Road Secondary Modern student who had been the victim of a sudden growth spurt. I didn't know much about The Hammonds at No 27 as the only son was quite grown up as far as I was concerned. I was content merely to designate them suitable targets for the ever popular game of Knocking On Doors & Running Away which was played with great enthusiasm whenever boredom set in. Mrs Hammond was known to use colourful language from time to time and Mr Hammond even chased me the length of Tooley Street one day for being rude to him which was terrifying and a little bit exhilarating. The Ribbens family lived at No 12 and were quite the most colourful family in the street. Vi, a tall, slim and eye catching woman, and her husband Sid were proud of their untidy brood of six good looking children headed by Young Siddy aka Daring Dexter. According to my mother the entire Ribbens clutch was both wilful and disorderly and would get into Trouble someday. However, even the unmanageable Ribbens boys generally managed to evade the attention of the local Police Force whilst my own brother, whose activities were theoretically far more controlled, did not.

Mr Ribbens wore a cap and worked diligently in some industry that ensured he returned home each evening looking as if he had been pulled through a coal mine backwards. Mrs Ribbens stood at her front door a great deal, greeting passers-by, and when she wasn't doing so made batches of toffee apples and hand sewed dresses for her oldest daughters, Angela and Sandra whose long hair was put into curling rags each night. Daring Dexter's younger brother was called Roger and the youngest two in the family were Jeremy and Sonja-Kim. Jeremy had been born with a disfigurement of one foot and ankle that was supposed to have regular treatment from the hospital. However, Vi opted out of the routine saying the poor little bugger's screaming broke her heart. My mother was somewhat predictably, affronted by this and told all and sundry, though not Mrs. Ribbens herself, that it Just Wasn't Right and that the Poor Mite Deserved Better! I liked Mrs Ribbens and when she presented baby Sonja-Kim to the street told her that I thought she gave her children lovely names. She looked at me as if seeing me for the first time and murmured that she had little enough to give the poor little blighters and so she liked to start them off with a really good name.

On one dramatic occasion young Roger Ribbens found himself on the front page of the local newspaper having carelessly fallen from top to bottom of one of the local chalk pits, a distance of one hundred metres, and escaping without injury. His mother was quoted as saying that the angels must have been watching over her little Roger, causing my own, ever critical, to make loud comment that Violet Ribbens wouldn't know what an angel was if she was to bump into one in the dark. It is probably fair to say that she disapproved of the poor woman perhaps for being too attractive or too indulgent with her children. Or maybe it was simply because she demonstrated a degree of affection for her family and disregard of what the neighbours thought that Nellie Hendy simply wasn't capable of herself.

Shepherd Street Shenanigans

Shepherd Street seemed a lively place where almost anything could happen and this was mostly because a large number of the roughest boys at St Botolph's School gave it as their address. It would never have been the first choice for a game of Knock on Doors & Run Away in case one of those boys happened to observe the activity and take it up at school the following day. We knew relatively few of the people who lived there, first and foremost because they were placed just a bit too far away from us for complete ease of brief chats over garden fences or at front doors for the adults. Apart from that it was a lengthy street of one hundred and thirty six small dwellings interrupted by just a couple of shops. One was the cobbler whose name I was only recently reminded of, a member of the Hammond family and he was there for years, mending boots and shoes the old-fashioned way and selling shoe polish and laces. The only other shop I remember in Shepherd Street was a general store run by Vic and Marguerite (known as Peggy) Troke who my mother was to later work for.

My classmate Kathleen Draper lived at number 64 and at 60 were the Philpotts, At number 69 were the Jenkins, one of whom was called Rita and a close friend of Doreen Lacey who I thought lived at number 67 but have recently been told came from York Road. Perhaps the Laceys at 67 were a different branch of the family or even a completely different lot of Laceys. In any event I recall Doreen and Rita, as a twosome, very well. They appeared to be Joined at the Hip as my Old Nan would say or Stuck Together Like Glue. I was more than a little envious of them. For one thing they both wore beautifully embroidered felt Dutch Bonnets, something of a fashion statement in headgear at the time whilst I seemed always destined to wear my mother's rapidly knitted and hideous woollen Pixie Bonnets that no self-respecting Pixie would have tolerated for a second. For another thing, they both at one stage were members of the same Brownie Pack as myself but earned far more badges and far more easily than I was able to do. Their Semaphore was, according to Brown Owl, quite superbly executed!

To be honest I wasn't much good at being a Brownie and my Aunt Mag said I'd never Taken to it. It had a lot to do with Doreen and Rita tormenting me about my home-made uniform on the way home in a manner that today would be described as a cut and dried case of Bullying and treated seriously. But back then victims of such harassment were simply advised to pull themselves together and fight fire with fire. The torment did not cease until I bit Doreen on the arm one day, quite hard. She was not at all happy and I remember a complaint being made to both Brown and Tawny Owls a few days later who jointly appeared to become faint with shock at the thought of biting in the ranks. Shortly after this incident I was not required to attend Brownies anymore which was an enormous relief.

To be more positive about Shepherd Street, a number of boy-heavy Dyke families proliferated in the area, not just in that particular street but in the more vague ones surrounding it and I remember at least two, Peter and John, in my class at school. Decades later when taking a holiday photograph of The Prince Albert pub at number 62, I met a female Dyke, a cousin or grand-daughter who was curious as to why anyone in their right mind would want to take photographs of back street beer houses.

The Prince Albert was first opened in 1855 and was immediately popular. During the post-war years it still did a thriving trade, especially on Friday and Saturday nights of course. Pearl Banfield who lived at the top of York Road became in the habit of directing her visiting boyfriends to the pub should they happen to need to use the lavatory whilst at her home. This was because she never wanted them to find out that it was situated in the outside yard.

The family that still stand out as memorable Shepherd Street residents were the Reads; Elsie and Les and their many children. Of their offspring I only clearly remember Jill and Jack who were probably the oldest two but there were certainly many more. My mother, predictably perhaps, spoke of them quite disparagingly saying they didn't wash their necks nor change their clothes from one week's end to another and describing Mrs Read as that-Elsie-Smith-that-was or: that Elsie-Read, her-that's-always-carrying. I envied the Read children their freedom to roam the streets long after dark and their early experimentation with cigarettes which they rolled themselves from gutter abandoned dog ends re-established with Rizla papers.

At one end of the Street there was a Baptist Chapel where children of any denomination were invited to attend Sunday School from three until four on Sunday afternoons. It was a popular activity with many of us because glasses of orange juice and ginger biscuits were handed out as well as transfers for the backs of our hands or arms depicting such uplifting scenes as Daniel entering the Lions' Den. From time to time coach outings were also organised to picnic spots like Cobham Woods or the village of Eynesford. Even we supposedly Roman Catholic children seized upon the generosity of these Baptists with enthusiasm and later thought, if indeed we thought about it at all, that we had been the fortunate recipients of an astonishingly open minded spiritual education.

Buckingham Road & Blasts from the Past

You could see quite a wide arc of Buckingham Road from our back gate, much more than the view we got of Tooley Street. It's only in recent years I've realised that the street itself actually bisected The Old Green, where houses no longer stood, and extended to the foot of York Road itself, probably even encompassing the unexpected little row of six dilapidated cottages that overlooked the Catholic School. We never quite understood in which road the cottages stood but although most of us fell firmly into the category of the Impoverished Poor, we were cautiously self-satisfied when we contemplated how much worse life could be if we lived in one of them.

Even in 1948 the cottages seemed to represent the kind of housing more commonly found a century earlier. Each consisted of two tiny ground floor rooms with a steep corner staircase winding up to two even smaller attic areas above. They had no running water and this had to be collected from a tap outside. Neither did there even seem to be gas lighting, the occupants all appearing to make use of oil lamps. Two lavatories serving the block had been erected close to the lower end of our own street and could be entered by a door adjacent to the alley that led directly to the front entrances of the York Road houses and provided a quick access through to Sims' Corner Shop. My mother often commented that she certainly wouldn't want to live like that and added that it would be easy for disease to spread. These observations were odd considering the even more disadvantaged conditions of her own early years but probably simply indicated that for the first time in her life she felt in a better position than someone else.

I no longer remember who originally occupied the end cottage where we practised ball games and hand stands against the side wall, but I do recall the flamboyant couple who replaced them. My mother told me that Myra had appeared on the Halls for years with her husband as a Magic Duo, performing tricks like Sawing the Lady in Half. For some reason we called Myra's husband, a bad-tempered man who clearly despised children, Treacle Pants. The exciting thing about this couple as far as my mother was concerned was that they were not simply tenants; they had actually purchased their cottage in 1950 for the grand sum of two hundred and fifty pounds. As this information spread through the neighbourhood Myra and Treacle Pants were accorded a certain amount of respect as befitted genuine property owners.

Next door to them lived the Stewarts who eventually had three children, Beryl, Julie and Richard. Beryl was not allowed to play with me since an unwise idea I had of swapping our new baby for their new baby which Molly said had been a stupid plan to begin with and she could never understand what made me think it would make anyone happy. She had of course been right. The Murphys lived next to the Stewarts with several children, one called Josie who was older than me and I don't remember much about her. At the end of the row were the Ships who had one child, a girl a year or two younger than me. Kathleen was outgoing and even though she was younger always seemed to be the bearer of interesting bits of information relating to the subject I had so recently been told must absolutely never ever be discussed again. Molly and I listened avidly whilst Kathleen regaled us with doubtful snippets of information about the number of her mum's friends who had somewhat surprisingly given birth to puppies or kittens. We always endeavoured to include Kathleen in games not only because of her remarkable though unusual sexual knowledge but also because her mother regularly made huge roasting pans of toffee which she broke with a hammer and distributed generously. Kathleen's father was a volunteer fireman and their kitchen had a device alerting him to when he was needed for fire-fighting. He would then most impressively speed off on his motorbike.

There were no shops in Buckingham Road but it did have its own pub, The British Volunteer which first opened in 1889 presumably when the houses were built. It was known locally as The Volley and well attended on Friday and Saturday nights when the piano that for years needed tuning and never got it, belted out the same catalogue of songs that everyone knew and in the same order. *Nellie Dean, Sweet Adeline, Waiting At The Church, A Long Way To Tipperary, Roll Out The Barrel, Show Me The Way To Go Home, Oh Mr Porter, Any Old Iron, Two Lovely Black Eyes* ... I could go on and on. Most of us living close to any pub where these numbers were sung vigorously on a regular basis became totally familiar with all the words and they still lie there in the sub-conscious needing just a few chords to jog them into life again.

The Dawson family lived at No 54 Buckingham Road although I was told the other day that they definitely lived in Tooley Street. Possibly there were two lots of Dawsons in the district, but the ones I knew had a daughter called June, an outgoing and well developed girl, a year younger than me and already importantly wearing a brassiere size 32 for the Junior Miss at the age of ten. June was rightly proud of this early step towards the world of adult women and keen to show the pink satin item of underwear to anyone who expressed interest. She self-importantly explained that she went with her mum the previous weekend to buy it from Marks & Spencers and it was definitely a size 32. I couldn't help feeling even then that a size 34 might have been a rather more prudent purchase because June was developing at a rate both fast and furious.

Beryl and Horace Ribbens lived near the pub and I imagine they must have been the in-laws of the Tooley Street family. Further down the street Ann Coppins lived with an aunt and uncle and although I played with her from time to time she was a reticent girl, always secretive about her family and sometimes saying she was not really supposed to talk about them. My mother described her as crafty and thought there might be madness in the family that needed to be covered up. Next door to her was a rather unfortunate child permanently confined to a wheelchair and said to be a cousin from Scotland. Her name was Elsie. She was very keen to be included in as many activities as possible and had an uncomplaining nature so that when various among us dragged her from her chair, convinced we could teach her to walk, she was always accommodating and valiantly pretended she was on the verge of doing so. At least once a week one or other of us would rush to her mother or grandmother urging them to come and look because we were totally confident Elsie was about to take a step or two unaided. She never actually did so.

The Bennetts lived at No 26, Frank and Grace with son, young Frankie and daughter Pat, both of whom were probably in their late teens and Little Joan who was my own age and much spoiled by everyone in the family. There had been a second son called Georgie, a year older than Joan, but he had died during World War Two following a nasty accident involving an air raid warning and a freshly made pot of boiling tea. Mrs Bennett was said to have never recovered from the child's death and was over protective of Little Joan as a consequence. Other people simply described Little Joan as Spoilt Rotten. When I was about eight or nine Pat Bennett married an Irishman called Mick, moved out to what had been for years an empty shop on the corner of Tooley Street and had a baby girl called Linda. All and sundry were advised by Mick who clearly disapproved of his in-laws and their neighbours, that under no circumstances was anyone to talk Baby Talk to Linda as he was keen to have her grow up speaking Proper English. Neither was Joan allowed to push Linda around the streets in her pram even though she was desperate to do so. My mother said it was because Mick couldn't stand the sight of Joan but that may have simply been to cover up the real reason which I always felt had something to do with my own baby-swapping activities which everyone seemed to be familiar with and reluctant to forget about.

The Bardoes lived at No 28, Wally and Eliza with their three boys, Kenny and a year or two younger, the twins Alan and Colin. Both Kenny and Alan were overtly macho boys who like to play aggressive games and neither of them at that stage of their lives at least, had much time for females. Colin on the other hand was a sensitive and insightful boy who not only greatly enjoyed playing with girls, but was a master at taking existing games and creating astonishingly creative twists. One entire summer, primarily choreographed by Colin, we played extensive Pony Club games although not one of us had ever been on a horse's back. Colin researched all the salient equestrian facts needed for the organisation of a gymkhana, even making silver cups by covering egg cups with foil and appropriating broom handles and old socks to form the basis of each individual steed. Mares and stallions were very soon lined up in a Buckingham Road abandoned Anderson shelter and the game continued for weeks. I cannot pretend it was totally popular with local housewives continually misplacing their garden brooms and the work socks from their washing lines. We were all very fond of Colin and it was with great sadness that decades later I heard via his twin brother Alan that he had died at a very young age.

It would be true to say that the children of Buckingham Road, like those of York Road and Tooley Street, had in many ways happy childhoods although I am certain we were a thorn in the sides of the adults around us, most particularly those who were childless or whose children had already grown up. The couple next door to the Bardoes undoubtedly came into that category because before the war they had made the significant and costly purchase of one of the earliest TV sets to become commercially available. When broadcasting resumed in

1947 they were of course inundated with requests for invitations into their front room to witness the extraordinary technology. If we were refused we simply jostled each other outside their front window, even standing on each other's shoulders to scrutinise the tiny screen to best advantage. It is unlikely that this long suffering couple enjoyed our fun-filled childhoods as much as we did.

Speaking of Springhead Road

There was once a definite feeling that those living in Springhead Road were a Cut Above the rest of us, and it's easy to see why because even these days the houses have retained an ambiance of solidity and permanence whereas many of those in the surrounding streets have gone forever. Back in 1949 the Springhead Road homes seemed very nearly elegant though you have to understand that this particular opinion arose from living on the long gone railway side of York Road and from the perspective of a nine-year-old. As far as I was concerned any home that was entered by a narrow entrance passage called The Hall was seen to be hurtling into the Upper Middle Classes. A bath that did not have to be detached from an outside wall every Saturday night spoke volumes about lavish comfort and I would have found Coronation Street's current inhabitants verging on upper class but of course they were destined to remain in the future for decades to come. My mother firmly proclaimed that where you kept your bath, whether outside or inside, didn't make you any cleaner than the next man but I think she missed the point.

As a teenager I was impressed that my first boyfriend, Barrie Wallwork, resided at No 10 Springhead Road in a solid looking flintstone house that I am certain had a Front Hall and a properly plumbed inside bathroom. I can't be totally sure about this because I never got further than the kitchen and that was on one solitary occasion because Barrie's mother was not particularly welcoming. My own mother was initially equally guarded about our relationship which was perhaps understandable as from memory I think we were only fifteen years old at the time of our Great Affair but she too admired the flintstone house and rapidly decided that I was unlikely to Do Better than he who lived in it. Years later I discovered from Barrie himself that the Wallworks were not actually the proud owners of the impressive Flint Construction – it had merely come with his father's job! At the time it mattered little to me because most people I knew were in rented homes and to be an actual property owner was something of an oddity.

The Scutts family lived at No 15 and I only remember Barbara who may well have been an only child. Several of the York Road mothers regarded her as Old Fashioned, a state that seemed to apply only to female children and generally went hand in hand with being either an only child or the youngest in the family. Barbara wore the kind of clothes that lesser mortals like myself greatly admired – angora boleros, smocked dresses, white socks, patent leather shoes and of course the inevitable fashion statement of the under twelves of the era, embroidered felt Dutch Bonnets. I both envied and disliked her but attempted to cultivate her friendship all the same because she was popular and I dearly wished to become part of the Smart Set. Accordingly when we played Call In Skipping Rope games (*Vote, Vote, Vote For Dear Old...?*) I always called Barbara into the rope and hoped she would remember the favour. She never did and in fact treated me with growing contempt. On one inauspicious day in a fit of showing off that wasn't repeated for a long time, I had an argument with her mother who said I was a Cheeky Little Cow and quite unexpectedly smacked my face. It was all to do with me insisting that I was not responsible for some misdemeanour concerning chalked drawings on the front steps of their Springhead Road house and furthermore that I had witnesses to prove it. She took exception to me using the term Witnesses. As I recall, my own mother reacted badly to the slap saying that I would no more tell a lie than walk on hot coals and that was a fact. There were threats to call the local Police which fortunately came to nothing and so the situation did not escalate further. After all the fuss died down it did not seem a good idea to admit that I had in fact actually been responsible for the much maligned art work.

Alice Gouge lived at No 24 and Mary Gouge who was presumably her daughter, went to St Botolph's School and was treated with more respect than the rest of us because her uncle was Sir Arthur Gouge and famous. We were not entirely sure what he was famous for but it seemed to be something to do with aviation. My father said I wasn't to confuse him with Landed Gentry because he was in fact only A Life Peer. I had no idea whatsoever what either of these terms meant and it was to be a long time before I could see the dichotomy involved in Landed Gentry living at 24 Springhead Road no matter how upmarket I considered the house to be in 1949.

Doris and Roy Snelling lived at No 40, relatives of my classmate Margaret Snelling who lived near the station at Northfleet and was to become a close friend for a while when I transferred to Northfleet Secondary School For Girls. She invited me to her nephew Philip's fourth birthday celebration, a great treat. Our family, large and diverse though it was, was definitely not big on observing rites of passage like birthdays. At Philip's birthday there was a cake in the shape of a train made by his grandmother. I was most impressed knowing that my own grandmother, Old Nan Constant, would have been both disinclined and incapable of producing such an exotic item. Shortly afterwards I went to yet another birthday event given by Jean Taylor's family who lived in the hastily erected post-war Prefabs in Meadow Road at the bottom of Springhead Road. Jean was best friends with Wendy Selves who lived in the other Prefabs close by in Orchard Road. Both girls were well behaved and diligent as far as school work was concerned and sported impressive ringlets. Fast becoming a more practiced party goer I took particular notice of the cake produced by Mrs Taylor Senior, iced as it was in pink and decorated with little silver balls, and told the gathered assembly that at my own birthday party my Nan had made me a cake in the shape of a mermaid with long green hair. Furthermore it had been completely iced in blue like the sea at Southend. Wendy Selves immediately said she didn't believe me and if it was true why didn't she and Jean Taylor get invited. There did not appear to be a convincing response to that question so I said nothing.

  The Campbells lived at No 42 Springhead Road with three daughters in their twenties, each of them a little immature. They were called Iris, Phyllis and Kathleen and two of them eventually ran the newly established Brownie Pack at St Botolph's Church that my mother, to my horror, still clinging to the idea that to join Brownies was a mark of respectability, suggested I might like to join. I dissuaded her by saying that both Phyllis and Kathleen Campbell had said I was too old and should wait a while and instead join Guides.

Fred and Ethel Finch lived at 79 where Ethel taught piano. Greatly admiring those children who entered her front door clutching their music cases, I took to sitting on the Finch front wall to listen whilst the students each belted out *A Carnival in Venice* mostly in a fairly pedestrian and unmusical manner. After a week or two Mrs Finch told me to move on and when I was slow to do so added that she had no time at all for the Undisciplined Kiddies from York Road and if I was not careful Mr Finch would have to call a policeman. And so I retreated and simply listened from a distance because sometimes when the lessons were finished for the day Mrs Finch herself would play pieces that I found strangely poignant and years later learned were Chopin waltzes.

83 Springhead Road was the site of Sims' shop where we bought newspapers, sweets and ice cream because it was in fact the closest shop to us, though my mother maintained she had never had much time for Hilda Sims and couldn't overlook her attitude with coupons during the war because there'd been no budging her. She did not explain further, however. No matter how little regard was afforded to Mrs Sims we had to admit that she was innovative and kept exciting stock. She was the first in the district for example to order in the new-fangled Ice Cream Suckers in various flavours even though they were threepence each and daylight robbery. My brother and I always knew that after a long day pea-picking down at Gemmell's Farm at the bottom of the

hill we might well be rewarded with an Ice Cream Sucker if we were especially non-complaining on the climb back home. The trek back up the hill with my brother in the push-chair clutching a bag full of pilfered peas to be shucked for our tea, was always a hard one. As we grew closer to Hilda Sims' shop, however, our spirits rose a little as we contemplated which flavour we might that day choose. Bernard, in his excitement loosening his grip on the soon-to-be-consumed peas, would whisper that today he was going to choose Strawberry and not Lime and my mother would tell him that if he didn't keep hold of them peas he'd be getting nothing at all. We knew that was just a threat though because the extra money earned that day of picking invariably stretched to a treat.

Further down Springhead Road on the left hand side before the railway overbridge and adjacent to the driveway into the Catholic School, a most unsavoury character lived with his wife and small daughters, though in a house that would certainly have had an inside bathroom. At least when we curiously scrutinized the layout of the rear of the place there appeared to be no zinc bath hanging anywhere. This was a man whose name is long forgotten and maybe I never knew it. Some people said he had once been a schoolteacher in one of the Medway towns but that claim may well have emerged simply from a desire to make a bad situation even worse. He was a large, untidy, gingery individual always wearing a grubby pale raincoat and much given to following small girls around the local alleyways, preferably as darkness was falling. Although he was renowned for this behaviour nobody had so far reported him to the local Police though we children were warned to hurry away if we found ourselves on the receiving end of this peculiar habit of his. This advice went unheeded a lot of the time because the excitement of leading him a merry dance around the local area was appealing. Once Molly and I managed to entice him into St Botolph's churchyard and with bated breath waited to see what would happen next. When he came close and actually spoke about a kitten he had in his pocket we took to our heels and ran off through to Church Path at the back of the school and reached home breathless and elated. None of this detail was ever shared with our parents of course. This miscreant in our midst was frequently discussed between the neighbours. Mrs Newberry from next door commented that it was his poor wife she felt sorry for but my mother was pitiless and said the woman seemed dozy to her and anyhow dozy or not she had made her bed and on it she would have to lie come what may even though there were little kiddies to be considered. The dozy wife and children were largely ignored in the neighbourhood and eyes were averted from all members of the family in Sims's corner shop where the man bought his tobacco or at Penny Son & Parker, the grocer on The Hill where his wife queued for cones of sugar and broken biscuits. There were of course no supermarkets at this time to add the slightest dimension of anonymity for those shoppers who might desire it, which given her husband's reputation she probably did.

    The rumour and gossip that attached itself to the gingery man was something that engrossed the neighbourhood and Molly said that it definitely had something to do with You Know What and her older sister Pam had told her that the man was trying to teach children how to French Kiss. Pam, being fifteen or sixteen years old was at the time the fount of all knowledge regarding that which took place between males and females. French Kissing, she maintained was quite normal if you were Going Steady, but absolutely forbidden if you were not. The process as described to me sounded so disgusting I was both silenced and chastened and shuddered at the very thought of Going Steady.

The London trains went under the Springhead Road Bridge and in those days all of them seemed to be steam trains. I recall now with ever mounting horror the game of First Across the Line is a Cissy and though this was a pastime largely confined to the older boys, foolhardy girls desperate for attention such as myself occasionally played it, presumably hoping to gain some kudos in the local child community. In my case I was rewarded with no esteem whatsoever and boys like Kenny Bardoe still looked disdainfully down upon me. Cat & Mouse games involving transport were, however, generally popular and I clearly remember the exhilaration of tempting the 495 and the 496 buses to dare to hit me when I dashed out in front of them as they gathered speed on the hill leading down to The Old Rec. The alarm on the drivers' faces was so gratifying and the rush of power so pleasing that this hazardous game was played again and again. Strangely the Recreation Ground itself was not considered to hold much worth as a play place, except with boys who wanted to kick balls, but the cemetery alongside it held far more possibilities and organised sessions of old-fashioned Hide & Seek were regularly held there and as we grew older, Kiss Chase also with the Bardoe twins. At the age of thirteen I became desperately keen on Colin who was always kind to me but clearly did not consider me romance material. Alan, on the other hand, was a different kettle of fish and once he reached his fourteenth birthday, he became enthusiastic for romance with any female showing the slightest glimmer of interest. Pat Turner complained that was the problem with Alan – he was always wanting to go Too Far. Colin on the other hand treated women with respect she said.

Pat lived somewhere at the bottom of Springhead Road and she was a pupil at the Catholic School but she came regularly to play with us on The Old Green and the back alleyways around York Road. Only a few years later she proudly became engaged to Colin, importantly communicating this information to us, looking very smart in a new red coat with a velvet collar and extolling Colin's virtues as a fashion advisor. I am told that finally the marriage did not actually take place which broke Pat's heart because she had loved Colin for as long as she could remember. Looking back on his many qualities it is easy to see why.

Aunt Elsie

The best thing about what we called Our End of Tooley Street throughout the 1940s and the early 1950s was Aunt Elsie's sweet shop at number 17 on the corner of the Old Green. Elsie Bull wasn't really anyone's aunt as far as I know but we all referred to her as such. She lived with Her George who nobody referred to as Uncle, in the end house where the front parlour had been turned into a shop and the window fitted with a smart wooden Venetian Blind that grew decidedly less smart as the years went by. The more elderly of the neighbours were sure that there had not been a shop at all on that corner back in the 1920s and that the business had emerged with the coming of the Bulls to the neighbourhood, from Margate or Ramsgate and why they had chosen to uproot and settle in Northfleet was a mystery. They did not appear to have a family but for a number of years a lodger called Joe lived with them and was said to be George's nephew though he looked too old to be entirely comfortable in that role. At times, particularly on Bank Holiday weekends when the shop was firmly closed, visitors crammed themselves into the back kitchen and the two upstairs bedrooms and on summer evenings drank beer in the back yard, sitting on planks supported by wooden fruit boxes. On these occasions there was a certain amount of jollity emanating from number 17 but other than that it was a quiet household with Aunt Elsie doing all the work because Her George only rarely appeared in the shop and my grandmother noted more than once that he must have been a Lazy Bugger all his life.

It's more than possible that tobacco products were also sold at number 17 because there was definitely a need to have a varied stock to get by on during the many years of sugar rationing, but I only recall the tall glass jars of Sherbet Lemons, Aniseed Balls, Bulls Eyes, Butterscotch and Hard Gums and I have no recollection at all of male customers requesting Hearts of Oak and Rizla Papers. One of the reasons for their general absence might have been because, unlike other local shopkeepers, Aunt Elsie never, ever served the adults in front of the children and was once heard to say to Grace Bennet that pushing the kiddies to the back of the queue was not a good way to run a business because like as not they always told their mothers. This was true of course and when this particular situation occurred in other shops, by the time I was twelve I had learned to point out as politely as possible that I had been there first. This was not always an unqualified success because some customers, mostly women, noted that I was a Cheeky Little Cow and if I wasn't careful my mother would be told exactly what I'd just said. After a while I so enjoyed the looks of irritation on their faces that I was likely to say it again just for the hell of it. But as I have said, this ploy was never needed in Aunt Elsie's establishment. By 1952, excitingly for her child clientele, the tall jars of well-known sugary assortments shared their shelf space with coils of Liquorice, Sherbet Dabs and Barratts Sweet Cigarettes and a little later with the new-fangled packets of Spangles and Polo Mints. It was fast becoming an exhilarating time for those with a sweet tooth.

So Elsie Bull remained our most preferred source of all the sweet items that were going to rot our teeth and generally we made our glass jar purchases two ounces at any one time and after a great deal of indecision. One of the compelling reasons for giving her our custom above any other similar outlet because she always waited patiently behind the counter for us to make our important decisions, staring at us unsmilingly from behind rimless spectacles, her bosom, ample for her small frame, often heaving and her breathing laboured. My mother said it was her opinion that she might well be harbouring TB though Molly's said it was probably only a touch of asthma and nothing to get too aeriated about. I chose to believe Mrs Freeman because she was not an alarmist. You could say that Aunt Elsie didn't go out of her way to be all that friendly but because she had been bequeathed with so much patience which she definitely needed with her youngest customers, she retained our loyalty. We would never have dared to keep Hilda Sims waiting for more than a few seconds whilst we made up our minds because she would not have tolerated it, neither would we have expected Peggy Troke to stand waiting whilst we debated the virtues of the available choices.

My brother when seven or eight years old was capable of standing lost in thought for several minutes at any one time before he could be persuaded to hand over the hot two pence clutched tightly in his hand, in exchange for a long rope of liquorice. On one momentous occasion however, quite uncharacteristically, he bought two Mars bars at fourpence each without much prior thought and even gave one to Hedley Davis who lived a few doors along from the shop. I knew at once that he had come by the money by foul means rather than fair and it had most likely been uplifted from my mother's purse. I failed to tackle him about it, however.

Aunt Elsie herself was a small dumpling of a woman of indeterminate age with red-brown hair, always half hidden under a hair-net. She invariably wore flowered smocks that hung loosely to her hips and fur trimmed slippers with slightly elevated heels that made her appear to topple forward as she walked. By the time we were twelve years old most of us were the same height as she was, the boys often towering over her as she weighed two ounce purchases with care and handed them over inside small white paper bags with the corners neatly twisted.

When she was on shop duty between the hours of nine and five, with a break at lunch time, we were all at liberty to use the long expanse of her side wall that bordered the Old Green for hand stand practice and improving our dexterity for the ball games that required a hard surface. To do so once the shop closed, however, was to invite the wrath of Her George who would appear promptly, red in the face and shouting at us to Clear Off, which we usually did.

By the time I was fourteen Aunt Elsie had died quite suddenly of a stroke and after a while the shop closed because Her George was disinclined to carry on the tradition of service to the public that she had initiated. It turned out that if she had not presented the warmest side of her personality to local children, he positively disliked every single one of us. We were strangely dejected when the slatted wooden blind came down for the final time and we wondered what might have become of the many jars of sweets. Molly said that it was always possible Her George had a reasonably sweet tooth himself.

Troke's Shop

There was very little similarity between Aunt Elsie and Peggy Troke apart from the fact that they were both shopkeepers. The Trokes lived in the cramped flat above their shop and it was situated at the other end of Tooley Street on the Shepherd Street corner.

Not one of us was aware at the time that Peggy Troke's real name was Marguerite because she was always known as Peggy, and sometimes just Peg. If we had known my mother would undoubtedly have thought her pretentious though she would have expressed this as being Up Her Own Arse which is not exactly fair as none of us are able to choose our given names. As it was she labelled her as flashy and no better than she ought to have been because it was rumoured that she spent too much time up in the flat with certain travelling salesmen.

Victor Troke, known simply as Vic, seemed not to concern himself with idle gossip and described his wife as An Angel and even gave her a beaver jacket for her thirtieth birthday making my mother snort and toss her head back in a strange gesture of general disapproval that was clearly supported by some of our neighbours. One of the reasons for this reaction was that apparently Peg was forty-five if she was a day. Quite apart from that, back in those days it wasn't a good thing to dress flamboyantly and be no better than you ought to be and furthermore Peg should really have had more sense than to court gossip by courting salesmen.

She was not popular with local children and did not have the patience of Aunt Elsie as far as her youngest customers were concerned. If we did not smartly make up our minds when comparing the attributes of Sherbet Dabs as opposed to Liquorice Wheels, she would tap her long red nails sharply on the glass counter top, purse her matching red lips and advise us to Get a Shuffle On. Generally speaking we only patronized the Trokes when Aunt Elsie was closed or when sent there on other errands by our mothers. On one occasion my occasional friend Greta Thilthorpe who was three years older than me and considered odd for wanting friendships with younger girls, reminded Peggy that as she was about to spend more than one shilling she would appreciate being accorded more courtesy. She made that statement in order to impress me, which indeed it did, standing at her side and hoping that the sweets would be shared – which they were. Furthermore Mrs Thilthorpe, always known as Tilly, actually worked part time in the shop which gave Greta a definite edge over any other youthful customer with an intention to be rude to adults. Peggy Troke said nothing in response but gave us both long and hostile looks when she placed the Polo Mints and Spangles on the counter with just a fraction too much force. As we wandered up Dover Road and into the grounds of the library, Greta told me that in her opinion Peggy Troke was just a bit too Big for her Boots and clearly thought she was a Cut Above the rest of us. Peg needed taking down a peg or two in her opinion – and sucking hard on shared confectionery I nodded enthusiastically.

Shortly after this exciting exchange my mother announced she was going to work for the Trokes one morning each week, not serving in the shop but doing Peg's housework to release her for more important tasks.

Despite her reservations regarding the general values held by her new employer, she seemed quite excited at the prospect and within a short space of time the relationship with the Trokes and their staff resulted in me becoming ever friendlier with Greta. It also occasioned the making of a red chiffon blouse for Greta's mother. I am uncertain about Tilly's satisfaction with the blouse since my mother's dress-making ability had not improved over the years but she was far too polite to complain and wore the blouse to her twenty-fifth wedding anniversary party to which we were invited. If you didn't examine it too closely it looked reasonably presentable worn with a great deal of chunky jewellery. Peggy and Vic were also at the event of course, arriving by car which Greta told me was an MG and Peggy very smartly attired in a pink tweed two-piece costume and a lace blouse.

Becoming more friendly with Greta, the only girl in the Thilthorpe family, meant becoming acquainted with her six good looking brothers, two of whom were of an age that interested me, particularly one called Michael who was sixteen and moody-looking in a manner that would have made even James Dean envious. At the time, as I was yet to stumble across James Dean who had in turn not yet embarked upon his short but stellar film career, Michael Thilthorpe emerged as a younger and more accessible version of Emily Bronte's Heathcliff and therefore highly desirable. Unfortunately for me he failed to notice my presence at all and the somewhat forced friendship with Greta began to pall despite her astonishing rudeness to adults, her sweet tooth and willingness to share.

It would be fair to say that my mother enjoyed the time she spent cleaning for the Trokes because the job seemed to provide a constant stream of minor scandal resulting in endless rumour and gossip in the neighbourhood, which could be commented upon and spread with ultimate efficiency. Peggy Troke bought far too many pairs of shoes apparently, and occasionally even drove down to Maidstone, where the shopping was legendary, in order to do so. She also went in for what she called Afternoon Dresses acquired from the newly opened Chiesmans Department Store in Gravesend and when the travellers called, she wore them in the morning if necessary. If she and Vic went out for their tea, which they certainly did from time to time, they drove into Gravesend to the Clarendon Hotel and ordered steak and chips. When the Berni Inn chain opened they became regular customers. Peggy once even persuaded Vic to take her to the new Pakistani restaurant near the bottom of Harmer Street but my mother failed to be impressed because nothing would have persuaded her to eat the kind of food foreigners seemed fond of. Vic said that he hadn't found it to his liking either if he was to be honest. Peggy ignored him and said she always had a gin and Dubonnet with her tea when dining out but Vic, bless his heart, always stuck to pints of mild. At around this time Peg began to describe going out for their tea as Going Out for Dinner.

The Trokes had a bob or two, there was no doubt about it because during those early years of the 1950s the shop did very well, hosting a constant stream of customers six days a week and they were quite adept at anticipating the buying needs of all, from the very poor to those who worked extra shifts at Bevans and were not doing badly at all. Grace Bennett from Buckingham Road, however, declared that one of the reasons for their success was that Peg was not beyond putting two fingers on the scale when weighing confectionery, especially when serving children who hadn't got the nous to notice. Her Joan, she said, was told to buy from elsewhere but of course when Aunt Elsie's was closed her Joan did what the rest of us did.

The majority of the customer base, living right on the Troke doorstep in Shepherd Street were very poor indeed and to their credit both Vic and Peg were capable of extending a friendly and helpful hand towards many of them. In fact Peg herself seemed particularly fond of the Reads, Les and Elsie who lived at 55 with their large mostly male family and when Elsie gave birth to yet another son expressed concern towards the only daughter, Jill, commiserating with her that a baby sister had not yet eventuated and handing over a few humbugs by way of consolation. She also showed unusual patience towards Brian Philpott from number 60 when he appeared with a collection of fast disappearing farthings in his hand enquiring the price of gobstoppers. This was, my mother said, because he was a Mongol and therefore lacking in understanding. The term Down Syndrome had not yet infiltrated among us. For some reason the Vandepeers at number 90 and the Baldwins at 122 did not inspire the same care and concern within either of the Troke breasts.

Quite the most sensational piece of gossip my mother was able to come up with during her time of employment was the confirmation that Peg was undoubtedly Carrying On! It had not escaped her notice that Derek, the traveller in stationery invariably made a monthly visit, as regular as clockwork and it almost always coincided with Vic's monthly visit to the wholesaler in Gillingham. Other travellers were scheduled in for quarterly visits, but although the shop sold far more confectionery and biscuits than birthday cards, for some reason the traveller in stationery called with unusual frequency. And what was more, decisions about writing pads were so complicated they demanded an unusual degree of discussion in the flat upstairs during which more than one glass of sherry and gin was drunk, never mind that it was only eleven in the morning. You couldn't pull the wool over my mother's eyes because she wasn't Born Yesterday.

It was shortly after the dissemination of this piece of information around the neighbourhood that Marguerite Troke, known simply as Peggy, came to the decision that she no longer needed a cleaner. My mother sniffed a lot and said she didn't really care because she'd been considering handing in her notice for a long time.

The Cobbler of Shepherd Street

Throughout my childhood and teenage years Mr Hammond was the person we took our shoes to when they needed mending because he was the local Cobbler and some people called him the Snob. Later on I learned that he was proficient in a wide range of repair services including watches and jewellery but our relationship with him only concerned footwear. He was an old-fashioned cobbler and at times was heard to claim that theoretically he should not be called a cobbler at all, but a cordwainer because he was a skilled artisan. Not so very long ago, he said, he had on a daily basis constructed luxury footwear and back in those days a cobbler was simply a person who repaired the shoes that men like him had made in the first place. And warming to his theme he was heard to add that back then the cobbler was actually forbidden from working with new leather at all and even had to use old leather for repairs. The difference between these two trades had once been considerable to the extent that to call a cordwainer a cobbler was to greatly insult him.

In Mr Hammond's opinion the long and proud British tradition of shoe-making was slowly but surely Going to the Dogs and this was because people no longer knew nor cared how their shoes had been made. It could only get worse he warned. None of this was of any interest to any of my aunts or my mother when they handed in items to be mended, the latter remarking that in her opinion he talked a lot of Twaddle which was probably on account of him being Chapel rather than Roman Catholic. She had never altogether trusted those who were Chapel. To be more honest she had a problem with anyone who was overtly religious.

When I was a pre-schooler my extra special black patent round-toed shoes with traditional ankle straps were handed over to this Cordwainer-turned-Cobbler simply to see if he was able to stretch them a little. I had outgrown them long before my mother considered it to be Normal and as they had cost a Pretty Penny and the soles showed evidence of a great deal of remaining wear, stretching might solve the problem. Mr Hammond was not enthusiastic and said that he had never been a big fan of stretching children's shoes because in the long run it did their feet no good at all. My mother's neck bristled with annoyance as she thanked him for his advice and she later told Mrs Bassant next door that not everybody was Made of Money and new shoes for children of my age not only involved expense but were hard to come by in wartime even if you had the required coupons. A few days later I inherited ankle strapped footwear that had once been red but were now a strange sludge colour, from my cousin Connie who lived in Waterdales.

Mr Hammond talked a lot and was said to be opinionated but no-one could say that he was not obliging and on occasions he went above and beyond the call of duty in service to the public. When my father came back from the war, later than his compatriots because of the debilitating illness he had contracted in North Africa, but looking hale and hearty once more, the first local shop he visited was Mr Hammond's. His black Sunday shoes needed attention if he was to attend Mass the next day at the Church of Our Lady of the Assumption looking his best. Cognizant of the importance of the situation, Mr Hammond did not allow his own religious affinities to stand in the way of his professional obligations and my father's shoes were attended to in record time causing him to remark to my mother that the Shepherd Street Snob was a decent chap. My mother did not respond except to sniff a bit but the good thing was that at eleven am Mass my father looked very dapper indeed in his pin-striped demob suit, white silk scarf and the newly mended shoes that shone to perfection. Mrs Judd whose husband had been Lost at Dunkirk, two of the Campbell girls and Sister Camilla all commented upon the fact that he was a very pleasant chap and it was good to welcome him back into the Roman Catholic community of Northfleet.

There was no doubt that Mr Hammond, despite his unfortunate association with Chapel, was a committed Christian. On a number of occasions when delivering footwear to him as we grew up, he would talk to me and my friend Molly about the life of Jesus, a topic that clearly absorbed him, and to a lesser extent also interested us. He was convinced that Jesus had visited Great Britain and probably even spoke English, perhaps almost as well as we did ourselves. When we exchanged glances and wondered how the Reverend Gunner at St Botolph's might view this information, he warmed to his theme and asked us if we agreed that Jesus would have been a strong and adventurous young lad. Molly nodded just a little doubtfully and Mr Hammond turned to me and wanted to know if I believed that Jesus was the nephew of Joseph of Arimathea. I nodded enthusiastically, anxious not to display my ignorance as to who this particular Joseph might be. Mr Hammond then became more animated because didn't this Joseph trade with the Tin Islands? Were not the Tin Islands the very land on which we now stood? Wasn't it plain common sense to accept that a healthy and venturesome young twelve-year-old lad would have been desperate to accompany his uncle on such an adventure? And wouldn't his parents have been delighted to allow him to go? Yes, yes, yes, we agreed, thrilled to think that Jesus Christ had as a boy perhaps trod the very same streets that we ourselves did! So thrilled were we that we lost no time in relaying the news to our classmates at St Botolph's only to find that The Reverend Gunner was less enthralled with the information. Later on I chose not to mention it at all to Father O'Connor or even to my own father.

The last time I remember calling upon the services of Mr Hammond was when I was twenty years old and had returned from a somewhat illicit period in Amsterdam in the company of a man who had assured me that he thought extremely highly of me but turned out to have a wife he was even more fond of in a suburb of The Hague. Although I had been forced to reluctantly relinquish him and the future we were going to have together, I was not required to surrender the very expensive shoes and matching shoulder bag he had bought for me in a pleasingly upmarket Amsterdam store.

The Cobbler of Shepherd Street was on my To Do list upon my return and I was more than pleased to be told that mine were the finest shoes Mr Hammond had seen in many a long year. Fashioned from the very finest leather, superbly crafted, they had been a joy to repair.

He recognised their excellence he told me because of course he had begun his working life as a cordwainer rather than a cobbler and not for the first time he carefully and at length explained the difference between those two terms. Not that there was shame in simply being a cobbler of course, he added, but over time the profession had become diminished and leant itself to less than perfect work. Standards had fallen everywhere. Which was of course, he said, half shaking his head as he handed the shoes back to me, what had led to that ungenerous term – Cobbling Something Together. I nodded, feeling sympathetic.

A Career In The Movies

It was some time in 1952 when my cousin Pat Doran, the only child of Aunt Martha, on a Sunday afternoon visit nonchalantly told me that a film company was about to make a movie on our very doorstep. She said she knew I'd be interested because I had told her months previously that my ambition was to be a film actress, well a film star to be more specific. Pat herself had no such ambitions and had already decided to apply for a job on the beauty counter in Woolworths and eventually work towards advising others which shade of lipstick might best suit them. When she told me about the film company she was quite casual because being a year older than me and more sophisticated by far, she knew she should feign complete disinterest in what was momentous news as far as I was concerned so she studied her pink nail varnish with an air of indifference. Looking back she was quite an actress herself.

Pat could generally be relied upon to be irritating and I didn't have much in common with her and on this occasion I could barely wait for her to leave before rushing two doors down York Road to inform Molly of the exciting news. We learned via the very next edition of The Gravesend & Dartford Reporter that the film was to be called *The Long Memory* and although the plot was detailed I've long forgotten what exactly it involved except that someone recently released from prison was keen on catching up with those responsible for putting him there. What I clearly recall is that it starred John Mills and Elizabeth Sellars both of whom were well known enough to cause us to gasp aloud because the idea of such hallowed beings deigning to tread the pavements of Northfleet and Gravesend was simply astonishing. I had a clear memory of John Mills in the lead role of *Scott of the Antarctic* which I saw with my father in 1948 and even thought I remembered him from *Great Expectations* some months previously although I had fallen asleep halfway through to my father's distress. Even my mother was impressed because she had seen him in *This Happy Breed* and thought he was a real gentleman and especially so in war films. She was extremely keen on films about the war even though she maintained that those years had ruined her nerves and nobody could ever know how thankful she was for it all to be over and done with.

As far as *The Long Memory* was concerned, very soon every second person was mentioning the filming that was about to take place in our midst so Molly and I decided to take a day off school to watch some of the scenes that were to be shot in Queen Street, Gravesend and The High Street. We didn't come to this decision without a lot of thought but in the end it seemed essential for our future planning. We told each other that we might well pick up vital tips for our careers. Once we had pledged one to another that what we desired more than anything else in life was to become stars of the Silver Screen it seemed unwise to the point of recklessness not to take advantage of all that we might learn from this film to be made almost on our doorstep. Molly pointed out that although the British Film Industry was of course important, what she would infinitely prefer was that her own career should take place in Hollywood. She had at that time an escalating obsession with Doris Day and felt it unlikely that Doris would abandon Warner Brothers for what The Rank Organisation might be able to offer her.

I wasn't nearly as fussy and nowhere near as preoccupied with Doris Day and had the Rank Organisation wished to sign me up I would have agreed on the spot. Once we had made the decision to abandon Colyer Road Secondary School for Girls for a day our most pressing problem seemed to be that notes needed to be provided for Miss Dennis the Headmistress. Miss Dennis was a great lover of notes and unlike some head teachers, seemed to read each one carefully. After much discussion I elected to write both notes, imitating as far as was possible, my mother's handwriting and that of Mrs Freeman which wasn't easy, and describing us both as Indisposed.

Subsequently we were able to head off for a tiring day in the lower part of Queen Street observing someone observing a house in an incognito fashion. The someone did not even appear to be John Mills himself but we were not absolutely sure of that because we could see so little of his face from the nearest doorway we had been able to organise to the action, which was mostly inaction. Molly had been hopeful that if we drew the cameraman's attention towards us we might be Discovered so she had spent some time singing *The Silvery Moon* and tap dancing along the pavement. This only resulted in a bored looking middle-aged man moving us even further along Queen Street. As we had spent our bus money on small cones of Papa's Ice Cream at lunch time, by four in the afternoon we were forced to walk home to Northfleet and on the way back it began to rain quite heavily which did nothing to improve what had turned out to be only a semi-successful day. It was all quite disappointing.

A day or two later we heard from Kathleen McCarthy whose parents ran The Queen's Head on The Hill that more scenes were to be shot even closer to home at the bottom of Granby Road in Northfleet. Kathleen had heard it from her father who had heard it from a regular customer. As Granby Road was home to Molly's newly married older sister Pam, we decided that rather than be forced to buy lunch time ice cream we might be able to prevail upon Pam to perhaps provide us with cheese on toast. It was from Pam that we discovered that the children from Lawn Road School were invited to watch the local filming and we were sick with envy because there was no chance whatsoever that Colyer Road Girls' Secondary Modern would be included in the invitation or even interested in becoming so. Under the circumstances and after discussion with Pam we felt almost obliged to absent ourselves from school for a further day and I again wrote the notes of explanation for both of us. Once more I described us as Indisposed which word I had learned very recently and had become rather fond of.

On this second voyeuristic occasion Molly decided that she would not put further effort into being Discovered because her singing and dancing might draw the attention of the supervising Lawn Road School teacher who may very well wonder who had given us permission to absent ourselves from our own school. Furthermore as those in the teaching profession were likely to stick together, that Lawn Road teacher might also turn out to be an acquaintance of our own Headmistress and then we would surely find ourselves in difficulty. This all seemed very sensible because you could never be too careful.

When the great day dawned, once again the several hours of watching nothing much happen from a distance turned out to be more tedious than we had anticipated. This was coupled with a certain amount of anxiety when we were spotted by a classmate's mother emerging from a nearby house who enquired curiously what on earth we were doing so far from the school gates on a Tuesday afternoon to which Molly smiled sweetly and said we had been visiting her sister and her new baby. In fact the new baby was not new at all being several months old but this explanation seemed to suffice for the time being.

Months were to go by before we were able to see the film at the Wardona in Northfleet and although we found the plot to be rather more involved than those of the Hollywood musicals and cowboy epics we were more accustomed to watching we found it highly exciting all the same and sat through it for a second time, quite riveted to the screen. The scenes on the riverside marshland, places we actually recognised, were stirring in their brooding intensity and quite suddenly places that had until then been ordinary and mundane became noteworthy in their appeal rather than tedious. Molly pointed out, however, that on balance she was still more drawn to Hollywood Boulevard or even Sunset Strip.

The unfortunate sequel to the two missed school days was that once Miss Dennis had actually read and absorbed the information in the bogus explanatory notes we were called before her for further clarification. She wanted to know exactly what our mothers had meant by saying that we were Indisposed. We were silent, giving the outer edge of the large blotter on her desk our full attention. She, however, was persistent. Were we perhaps experiencing difficulty with our monthly periods she wanted to know. Astonished by the casual manner in which this silver haired woman in her pale blue twinset spoke with so much offhand precision on a subject that our mothers would have only mentioned in whispers, we blushed to the roots of our hair and remained mute, heads bowed, eyes now directed towards her feet.

Miss Dennis seemed to take this reaction as a definite Yes and gave us each a brochure to read called *Adolescents Coping with Period Pain*.

Huggens' College

Aunt Queenie, my hermaphrodite Aunt who wasn't really an Aunt at all but a cousin on my grandfather's side of the family, was exceptionally keen to be accepted as a resident of Huggens College, or at least that is what she said. Not unexpectedly in the final analysis her application was turned down. My mother said it was because of her unresolved gender, though she didn't express it quite like that. Great Aunt Martha who lived in Hamerton Road maintained that the place was for more middle class and educated persons who were regular church-goers and the indecision about whether any applicant was male or female would not have come into it but she wasn't quite right there. My Grandmother said that far be it from her to spread rumour and gossip but if she had been inclined to do so she could tell a story or two about Queenie that would have prevented her ever entering the local fish and chip shop, let alone Huggens College. I wondered what on earth could be so very special about the place, sitting as it did behind what seemed impenetrably high walls. The only people we ever saw coming and going, apart from delivery vans, were elderly ladies carrying shopping baskets or bunches of flowers and walking slowly though purposefully along the High Street.

Until I became friends with Brenda, the oldest daughter of my father's foreman at the Cement Works, I had never been inside the place but I was increasingly curious as to what might lie behind the rather intimidating exterior. From what I could glimpse of the Gatekeeper's Lodge, I began to rather fancy living there myself. Once the friendship with Brenda was established I did not have long to wait because her family had a relative in residence who was definitely anxious for visitors. I got to know Brenda at a time when my mother was particularly keen on me making what she called Proper Friends by which she meant those girls who went to Sunday School and belonged to Brownies. This wasn't as easy as she might have imagined because usually those with a taste for religion and doing good deeds avoided me which I didn't mind because they were not especially interesting. It was remarkably easy to become Brenda's friend because she was not particularly likeable and of a highly nervous disposition which gave her mother concern for her welfare whilst greatly desiring she should make friends with other girls. She would have preferred Nice Girls but in the end settled for me.

Before long she and I found ourselves visiting her Great Aunt Lavinia together with a basket of vegetables from Brenda's garden. I was pleased to find that once inside, Huggens College was pleasingly reminiscent of Days Gone By and I felt that we should really be wearing the kind of clothes favoured by Mary Lennox in Frances Hodgson Burnett's *The Secret Garden*. I mentioned this to Brenda but she said she'd never read it and asked me why I was whispering. In fact it was a place where whispering came easily, feeling as it did just a little like entering the cloisters of a significant cathedral. I suggested perhaps playing a game where we pretended to be book characters from long ago but it turned out that Brenda was not really much of a reader and was even dismissive of Enid Blyton which was surprising in 1952 and rather shocked me.

The forty or fifty tidily identical little houses seemed to be built to form a square and they were surrounded by exceptionally well-kept lawns and gardens. From memory, a further wing faced the river down to which the whole complex gently sloped. There were rows of horse chestnut trees against the walls which I noted would come in very handy should the residents have an urge to play Conkers later on in the year. Though of course the game, mostly favoured by boys, was not one that generally appealed to adults.

Aunt Lavinia looked as if she was expecting us and immediately poured glasses of her home-made lemonade which was completely different from any version I had previously experienced and to be honest not entirely to my taste. She was a small plump woman wearing a long muslin dress and a little white lace cap making her similar in appearance to Great Aunt Martha of Hamerton Road. Her little house, sitting as it did alongside the hustle and bustle of Northfleet High Street, yet clearly quite apart from it, was to my mind rather like a fairy-tale cottage. It had an enticing porch entrance into the living room and a kitchen that I believe must have been equipped with a bath because I don't recall a bath anywhere else. A narrow staircase led up to the bedrooms, the smaller of which our hostess told us was originally intended for maids or companions as so many of the earliest residents preferred not to live alone.

I decided to ask how she came to be living in such a lovely place and if it was totally necessary to be well educated in order to do so. She explained that the cottages were in fact an estate of almshouses, a term that was new to me, and had been built to accommodate those ladies of the High Anglican Faith who were of unblemished character and found themselves in Reduced Circumstances. I didn't like to ask what she meant by that because it sounded like something I ought to know about so I just listened. She said that one of her mother's cousins had in fact been a Founder Resident as long ago as 1848 when the College first opened to receive those who met the entrance qualifications. Back then each resident was allocated a monthly allowance along with a ton of coal each year. John Huggens the instigator of the idea was a wealthy corn merchant and philanthropist from Sittingbourne and originally the College was going to be built there but try as he might he simply couldn't get the required permission for the venture no matter how great his financial resources were. It was that misfortune and difficulty that became Sittingbourne's loss and Northfleet's gain! He was said by some to be an abrasive and difficult man but ultimately became extremely well thought-of because he had not only provided homes for the elderly Anglicans but also a chapel with a cottage for the vicar and a croquet lawn for those who enjoyed the game. At the mention of croquet I pricked up my ears because although I had never played the game in my short life and the only thing I knew about the rules was what I had gleaned from Lewis Carroll, it sounded like a splendid opportunity for an extended fantasy that might last for days. It seemed a pity that Brenda was a playmate so lacking in imagination.

Aunt Lavinia went on to say that originally there had been a statue of John Huggens over the main entrance gates but that had to be taken down during the Great War for fear of it falling on someone which was just as well when one considered the bombing we had all suffered during the next war. Later on the gateway itself had been struck by lightning and had to be repaired so henceforth the main gates were only used occasionally and residents and visitors alike were required to enter via one of the smaller entryways in College Road. Of course, she said, a funeral was different and the main gates were always opened on those occasions even though they were inclined to stick.

She showed us a photograph of John Huggens sitting in an armchair with eight stern looking women around him that she said had been taken when the first cottages were pronounced ready for occupation. Then she showed us another photo of his funeral procession which had apparently been one of the most impressive ever seen in Northfleet or possibly even Gravesend as well with a hearse drawn by six plumed black horses and a young man walking before them holding a canopy of ostrich feathers. She told us he was buried in St Botolph's Churchyard and there had been coach after coach of mourners all dressed in black and that after a month or two a Board of Trustees was appointed to run the College. It was said that the Board was not nearly as efficient as Huggens himself had been and the monthly allowance and allocation of coal soon stopped which not everyone had approved of and subsequently there had been rumour and gossip. By the time we were acquainted with all this information about the rather saintly benefactor it had become totally clear to me that poor Aunt Queenie would never have made an entirely suitable resident and I felt a twinge of regret because it was clear she would have very much enjoyed living in one of the little houses. My brother and I would have definitely appreciated visiting her and perhaps even learning to play croquet whilst she made tea and chatted with our mother. For at least the next year I harboured a longing to live in one of those fairy tale cottages and sit each evening observing my neighbours from behind a lace curtain.

Years later when attending the first wedding of my then almost adult brother I learned from one of the guests that the pretty little almshouses I had admired so much had been rather unwisely built from Kentish Ragstone which was said not to have weathered well. The speaker obviously found that hard to believe saying that it had been used locally for over a thousand years and in fact was the hardest rock in the county. After all neither local churches nor Leeds Castle were in danger of disintegrating were they? It was his belief, the guest said, that there was Much More to it than simple wear and tear of Ragstone. And of course he may well have been right. Nevertheless by 1966 Huggens' original College had been largely torn down and a new, smaller complex built in its place with the promise of a brand new chapel but no sign whatsoever of a croquet lawn.

Apparently ten acres of the formerly pristine grounds had been sold to the local council who built flats for pensioners there and named the venture The Wallis Park Estate. In 1969 my mother moved into one of them and with memories of the Huggens College Almshouse still fresh in memory, was excited to do so, leaving 28 York Road behind her without a backward glance. Sadly the move was not a happy one with the delinquent behaviour and vandalism of bored local teenagers almost impossible to put up with. She was more than happy to move on to Pickwick House on the Painters Ash Estate a year or so later.

At the time I could quite understand the ease with which she left Northfleet. When I had visited her at Wallis Park I found the rapid local changes made it almost impossible to recognize the area as the environs of the old High Street that I had known so well as a child. College Road, Samaritan Grove and Hive Lane all seem to have evaporated along with the myriad of familiar shops and businesses. The last vestige of bygone days was a block of flats called Rayners Court which presumably had been named in honour of the local family of Rayners who had run the hardware store with such fortitude and determination for so many years. It always seemed a great pity to me that the Kentish Ragstone so favoured by John Huggens had weathered quite as badly as it did.

A Decent Friendship at Wombwell Hall

As I've said previously, I was never the kind of child who was good at making friends. It can be quite demoralising to always be standing on the outer edge of cohesive playground groups, at best tolerated but never accepted. That's not to say that I was entirely friendless because that simply wasn't true but generally those who were comfortable with me were not entirely accepted themselves. This fact was not overlooked by my mother, always more astute than she appeared to be, who many years later insisted that it was because I had a Quarrelsome Nature. She firmly believed that those of my ilk were destined to walk alone and as I was at that stage largely unaware that I was the author of my own misfortune there seemed little that could be done about the situation.

In my last year at St Botolph's Primary School I became more friendly than was usual with Pearl Banfield, who lived at the top of York Road and whose mother was particular regarding those with whom her children associated. It was clear she was apprehensive about me and that was possibly because of Aunt Freda and the black market stockings that were never delivered in 1943. Her attitude became even more entrenched after I wrote the unfortunate poison pen letter when Pearl passed the eleven plus and I didn't. Unsurprisingly that really put the cat among the pigeons and naturally enough Pearl was to have nothing further to do with me. Under the circumstances even I understood this stance although I think Pearl would have been happy to forgive me.

I wasn't too upset because I had taken the precaution of becoming more than half friendly with Margaret Snelling who lived close to Northfleet Station and who let me have rides on her new bike. Our friendship declined somewhat when we transferred to the local secondary modern school and eventually found ourselves in different streams. I had been placed, somewhat surprisingly considering my abject Eleven Plus failure, in the A Stream. Margaret was a B Stream Girl even though she was much better than me in all aspects of Arithmetic, even long division. I thought a mistake had been made and in the first week or two worried a great deal about Arithmetic now more terrifyingly called Mathematics and how soon it would be before it was discovered that I had not grasped the basics in this subject. I worried so much that I might even have approached the Headmistress, Miss Dennis, if only she had not chosen to have her office beyond reach in the Senior School which was situated rather inconveniently at least half a mile away.

Miss Dennis of the silver hair and pale blue eyes held an assembly in the Junior School only once a week and talked about Being Happy at Work and Play and Striving to Do One's Best At All Times. Her Tuesday morning homilies were exceedingly dull and a bit like listening to Father O'Connor's Sunday sermons; in fact he might even have been rather more interesting.

Molly from number 31, who was in the year ahead of me had been highly excited when she first went to Northfleet Girls' Secondary Modern and said it was exactly like being at boarding school except you didn't of course sleep there. You were allocated Houses, she told me and she was a Dame Laura Knight girl and for certain events like Games for instance, you wore a coloured sash that indicated which House you represented. Dame Laura sashes were blue. There were Prefects who stood in the corridors and penalised students for not walking properly or being too talkative and she was very much hoping to become one. I found myself in Helen Keller House and wore a yellow sash and knew for sure I was not destined to ever become a Prefect.

The two years at Northfleet Girls' passed in a remarkably uneventful manner. The only spike of interest was when Mrs Rowntree the History teacher proposed that we each make a reproduction of the Bayeaux Tapestry. However, it turned out to be merely a suggestion and I was the only one who acted upon it which caused a great deal of merriment among the group of twelve-year-olds who were at that time my loose associates. Shirley Monroe even asked me if I was trying to become a Teacher's Pet which I vehemently denied. Even the English classes were tedious and I must have somehow coped with Mathematics, probably by trying hard not to draw attention to myself.

I don't recall how it happened but somehow or other I was selected for a possible place at Wombwell Hall. I say possible because my entry depended upon an interview with the Headmistress, Miss Fuller. The idea of Wombwell Hall was infinitely more exciting than anything that had gone before and from the moment I first stepped inside the old house it wrapped itself around me and I fell deeply in love with the place. To me the school, humble technical college though it was, had a solid reality about it and seemed to be a Real Place of Learning with staff that were decidedly more dedicated than I was accustomed to and one or two of them ultimately proving to be quite inspirational.

My mother was also impressed and said that if I played my cards right I might find it was the kind of place where really Decent Friends could be made, not fly-by-nighters like Pearl for example or even that Snelling girl with the bike. I was wholeheartedly in favour of Decent Friends and vowed to become a much friendlier person, accommodating and co-operative in order to attract the exceptional human beings who would undoubtedly change my life for the better.

I met Yvonne from Swanscombe on day one, a tidy and confident girl wearing a hand knitted dark green cardigan almost a mirror image of my own, rather than the costly regulation version from the Uniform Shop in Gravesend. She also sported a well-worn brown leather satchel rather too large for someone of her small stature. We stood side by side at the first Assembly and she told me that she was delighted to be given what she called This Important Chance because her father had died a year or two before and he had really cared about her education. She was exceptionally keen to become a copy typist. I could have hugged her because suddenly, here before me was another Fatherless Girl, and very likely a Really Decent one. I decided there was already an important link between us and with a modicum of luck in no time at all we could be best friends. At long last my cards had been played right!

We sat together, Yvonne and I throughout that day and in fact for the whole of the first week. She even shared her morning break ginger biscuits with me and told me the details of the workplace accident that had taken the life of her father and how her mother was now really struggling to ensure that she and her younger sister, Doreen, were raised properly. In fact Yvonne said things that made me positively glow with a quiet serenity even though there were aspects of her personality that were just a tiny bit tedious. It was this little corner of tiresomeness that led to me being almost relieved when a third girl was instructed to join us in the first Friday Science Experiment. Valerie Goldsack who had golden hair to match her golden name sat between us and had a lot to say for herself because her father was a Detective Inspector in the local Police Force. Her father's position and the kudos it afforded her made her a bit of a Know-All which became almost immediately obvious. At the conclusion of the science class to our delight we found that our little trio had won the Prize of The Day for our work which was primarily because Valerie had already completed the experiment at her previous school. Nevertheless we were gratified by our success and unlikely though it was I even began to wonder if I might have an aptitude for science as I did not seem to have an aptitude for anything else. The prize was a small bar of Frys' Mint Chocolate each. As we got ready to go home I made rapid work of demolishing mine. Yvonne ate half of hers and said she would save the rest for her sister. Valerie, looking disapprovingly at me as I discarded the blue and silver wrapping in the waste paper basket, said she was saving all of hers for Daddy because Daddy really liked Frys' Mint Chocolate. Apparently it was his favourite treat.

I was unsettled on Monday morning when Yvonne suggested we invite golden haired Valerie to join us at morning break. By Wednesday I became further perturbed when Valerie produced her mother's fairy cakes to supplement the ginger biscuits. To my later humiliation I was even reduced to tearful and infantile objection which caused the now hated Golden One much amusement.

By Friday they were sitting together in class, sharing secrets and laughing at each other's jokes. Oh how rapidly I had been relegated to the extreme outer rim of the Decent Friendship. Subsequently it also transpired that I had also been quite wrong about having an aptitude for science.

The Two Miss Smiths

There is no doubt at all that I felt completely at home the moment I stepped over the threshold of Wombwell Hall in July 1953 for the Entrance Assessment Interview. It was as if I had a residual memory of a past association with the place. This was of course both fanciful and ludicrous depending upon your viewpoint. Nonetheless the very walls seemed to envelop me in security and warmth and I knew immediately that each and every part of the old house would become an invaluable aid to the various lives I lived in my imagination, most of which were in no way connected to everyday life and lacklustre reality. Daily I could immerse myself in the intricacies of a BBC historical drama or even a Rank Organisation mini epic, of that I had no doubt.

I was not an especially creative child, nor an original thinker and there was nothing I did particularly well but I was filled with an insatiable and secret desire to somehow escape from my place at the bottom of the Social Heap in the Victorian industrial terraces of Northfleet and Gravesend. My ambition was not to become overly rich but merely to excel in some aspect of the creative arts such as Drama, Dance or Music. Perhaps even write stories that others would read and be inspired by or possibly even scripts for films or television. These aspirations, disconnected from reality though they were, did not diminish as time passed but grew ever stronger. To be fair they had been made a great deal worse by the Children's Department of Northfleet Library and the obsessive reading and re-

reading of Noel Streatfield books featuring troupes of child actors and dancers who all seemed to achieve celebrity with remarkable ease. Taking a break from Streatfield I became enthusiastically immersed in Pamela Brown's Blue Door Theatre stories where neighbours living in an ordinary town in the South of England launched their own successful repertory theatre. If they could do it, why couldn't I? The book characters were not particularly well off, the authors had gone to some pains to point this out but it was manifestly obvious that they were decidedly Middle Class and often their described Poverty could be firmly placed in the ranks of the One Servant Poor variety. In those years that followed the end of the War, coming from a Working Class background still held a great deal of stigma as far as progress through various career options. My own family circumstances made the Decent Working Classes look not only respectable and virtuous but also positively prosperous. I was very keen that my situation should at some stage, somehow or other change for the better. It might well be that Wombwell Hall could be the catalyst for this.

Happily it was being an Eleven Plus Failure that led to me finding myself there in the first place. When we got the good news that I had secured a place at The Local Technical School For Girls and my maternal grandmother, Old Nan Constant, had finished berating my mother for what she saw as the folly of Getting Involved With Yet Another Bleeding Senseless Highfaluting SCHOOL If You Don't Mind, we went on the bus to Waterdales to visit Aunt Lou and Cousin Connie from my father's side of the family. My cousin had been a Tech Girl for a year and would not only be able to fill me in with all the important details about the place but more importantly, be able to pass on her outgrown uniform.

When I finally began my first term in September that year I had firmed up considerably on my ideas about a career and sensibly decided that I needed to give more than cursory attention to shorthand and typing, not because I had any real desire to fulfil my mother's dream that I should become a shorthand typist which was a Nice, Clean Job where no hands became dirty in the execution of it, but because such skills might well prove useful to me if instead of actually starring on the West End stage I instead opted to write the epics for others to star in. I wouldn't be the first successful writer to master Shorthand. You only had to look at Charles Dickens and it probably wouldn't have been beyond him to also become an accomplished typist which would have saved him a great deal of time, especially when you considered how long some of his novels were. I struggled to find other writers who could definitely write shorthand and type but this was long before Google and information was thin on the ground although I did stumble across Samuel Pepys briefly. At thirteen years old I found him boring and slightly scary and quickly decided it was doubtful if he was an aficionado of Isaac Pitman. Also he didn't seem to quite be able to write Proper English which seemed odd to me at the time when you took into account how well known he seemed to be and how well regarded by some people who obviously didn't mind being bored. Much later he was to become almost like a friend, so obsessed did I become with the diaries.

During my first few weeks at Wombwell Hall I was so completely captivated by the place that I spent a lot of time attempting to ensure that I would be the last student to leave a room in order to absorb as much of the information from the past that still lingered in the walls as humanly possible. I trailed my fingers over windows and wondered if the glass panes were the very same as those fitted one hundred years previously or if any had been replaced because someone was careless when playing Cricket. Sadly very little of this enormous enthusiasm I had for the house itself ever transferred into academic excellence of a general nature and I was for the most part a rather less than average student which my school reports definitely indicated without any doubt whatsoever.

Although I was doing reasonably well in the commercial subjects in that I managed to hover around the middle of the class, I cannot honestly say I enjoyed what I was doing and the same went for most other subjects. History and Geography were both more than dull and Science became equally arduous. I was totally hopeless at any kind of sports and generally quite frightened of taking risks and getting hurt although I could just about tolerate an occasional gentle game of hockey as long as I was allowed to play Right Wing which seemed to be the easiest and most stress free position on the field. Mathematics remained a hated mystery and French followed very closely behind, always threatening to overtake. Both subjects kept me awake at night as I fearfully contemplated how I could make myself invisible in the following day's classes.

I remember very few of the teachers really clearly because it was first and foremost the house itself that fascinated me. Miss Hart who reigned over Commercial Subjects still stands out because she was an eccentric character and hard to dislike. Furthermore she had an interesting wartime career in which she flew planes. I recall a little about Miss Springate whose subject was Geography and who always looked old and careworn, except that she clearly didn't like me and this might have had something to do with my complete lack of interest in the Nile Delta. I remember more about Miss Eatch, a History Teacher, because when she first came to the school she was so nervous I brutally manipulated a spiteful campaign to make her cry by the end of each lesson and rejoiced when she became our Form Teacher and could be further persecuted. Miss Norman, who taught Science, was also our Form Teacher for a year but I recall nothing about her except she may have had a Northern accent and she was appalled that we seemed to know nothing about Romney Marsh Sheep which she described as our very own Kentish Variety. I did in fact know something about them from my reading of Monica Edwards books where Romney Marsh children had one adventure after another involving horses and frequent mention of sheep. It did not seem sensible to bring this up, however.

There were though, two members of the staff who still stand out with extraordinary clarity: the Miss Smiths! Miss S and Miss K who appeared to rapidly develop a close friendship demonstrated by their frequent walks around the grounds together during the lunch breaks, sometimes with arms linked, heads down and always deep in conversation. Valerie Goldsack who was definitely less naïve than the rest of us sniggered and said they were Women in Love. I, along with the majority of Form 2SC, had absolutely no idea what she meant. Miss S Smith was already at the school when I arrived in September 1953 and in fact was my 1SC Form Teacher for the first two terms. She taught both Games and French and because I found the former unbearably threatening and the latter unbearably challenging I tried as far as possible to make myself unnoticed within her classes and speak as little as humanly possible. On my school reports she seems to have regarded me as lacking in confidence which I probably was and even if I wasn't, to be thought so was fine with me. The rather more wonderful Miss K Smith suddenly turned up at Wombwell Hall in the September of my second year and she taught only English. She was a quite superb and inspirational English teacher. That's not to say that my marks in the subject suddenly rocketed sky high under her stewardship because they seem to have hovered perpetually around B minus which I still find a little disappointing. But despite my average performance there was no doubt that Miss K Smith opened the door for me into a world of words I had not previously appreciated. She even gave me advice regarding having one of my short stories published but I now cannot remember what that advice was. In her class I did not hide among the sea of desks hoping not to be noticed but instead generally paid attention, was even industrious and actually tried to please her by producing what I fervently hoped she would think was commendable work.

My ambition at the age of fourteen had crystallised yet further and manifested itself as a burning desire to simply become famous. If I had to achieve that renown by producing Best Sellers then that's what I would do, especially if it meant the approval of Miss K Smith, but it didn't mean I had completely abandoned the desperate longing to also reach the dizzy heights of celebrity via Stage or Screen. As an ideal I tried to model myself on the Great Sarah Bernhardt followed by Dame Edith Evans but because my only experience of Live Theatre had been a single visit to the Christmas Pantomime at Chatham Empire, to keep the fantasy alive I was often reduced to lesser mortals such as Doris Day, Grace Kelly or Kim Novak all of whom I was much more familiar with from occasional cinema visits with Molly from 31.

Overall I decided that Acting would be in the long run probably more satisfying than Writing, though there seemed no real reason why I should not attempt both. Furthermore a career on the stage would undoubtedly prove less intensive than all that writing late into the night. From what I could gather from the monthly Film Magazines purchased by Molly's older sister Pam, once you achieved a certain level of Screen Stardom and became a household name, there was also a great deal of wining, dining and general socialising with other celebrities that took place not just in London but also in Paris, New York and Los Angeles. I was certainly keen on the idea of all this and during French Double Periods even planned my required wardrobe for these glittering occasions. It featured a number of silver and gold lamé sheath dresses, strappy high heeled sandals and stockings with butterflies adorning the seams as well as a fur stole that I thought might well be Arctic Fox. At that time I had only a hazy idea as to the general appearance of Arctic Fox.

Because of my reading diet I still daydreamed constantly of somehow enrolling in a Stage School such as the Italia Conti school in Soho which I was sure would not only act as a launch pad for my stage or film career but also allow me to tap dance into the footlights via West End Musical Comedy productions. I was not entirely averse to the idea of the occasional Classical Ballet performance at Covent Garden also. I was completely undeterred by the fact that I had never attended a single dance class of any description and convinced that I would easily pick up the necessary skills when the time came. In the interim and to be on the safe side I did borrow a book from the library concerning basic ballet steps and positions and from time to time practised them in the privacy of my bedroom.

Very occasionally I foolishly brought up the subject of a stage career with my mother who simply looked at me in amazement and told me not to be So Bloody Daft. Once when the topic was spoken of in the presence of my grandmother I was advised that No Bugger Would Pay Tuppence to Watch a Great Nora Like Me, which was disheartening to say the least. But the desire for fame and fortune via the Arts did not diminish and was still burning as fiercely as ever when I reached my fifteenth birthday, although the threat of approaching mid-year assessments concerning Pitmans and Typing Speeds meant a modicum of attention had to be paid to achieving these skills. Miss Hart thumped the desk and with her warning boom voice alerted us to the dire possibility of not being Good Enough for a Gravesend Office so we all knuckled down.

I drifted through the upper floors of Wombwell Hall during lunch breaks, always alone and at times totally absorbed with the idea that I was taking part in a BBC production of Wuthering Heights, staring out of windows and turning the school gardener into Heathcliff with ease, feeling ever more alienated from my peers, all of whom seemed to accept the office future that was neatly mapped out for them. Increasingly desperate to confide in someone who might not only be helpful but also be impressed with my hopes for the future I at last decided to make Miss K Smith the recipient of my confidence. She often spoke about the theatre, told us how wonderful it was to go to performances at The Old Vic, urging us never ever to overlook William Shakespeare. Anxious for her approbation I had already learned half a dozen of his sonnets by heart desperately hoping that she might at some stage ask the class if anyone was Familiar with them. Had she done so I would have gladly forsaken Musical Comedy and Ballet forever for a place in the Old Vic Company. So far she had disappointed me but surely once I fully acquainted her with my lofty ambitions she would undoubtedly see me as a kindred spirit and take me under her wing. Who knows I might even get to know her well enough to share a Saturday morning assignation over cups of Nescafe at The Copper Kettle, the stylish teashop in Cobham Village where Valerie Goldsack and her mother had noticed her one weekend. That's if Valerie could actually be believed of course and you could not always depend on her.

I waylaid Miss K after a Double English Period when the rest of 2SC were rushing off for a Wednesday pre-lunch game of hockey. She and I were all at once alone together in the room that had been the Library of the old house. She wore a beautifully ironed white shirt under a beige Pringle cardigan. I had noticed the label in the cardigan a few days previously when she took it off and threw it carelessly over the back of a chair. I made a note then that at some stage I would somehow or other acquire a similar garment. It was without doubt a cardigan that those familiar with Shakespeare Sonnets might wear with not a whiff of Marks & Spencers or British Home Stores about it.

She smiled kindly and asked what she could help me with. Verging on tears I said I was going to tell her an important Secret and would she please never discuss it with others. I implored her for advice. How could I become an actress because that was what I wanted to do more than anything else in the world? And she didn't laugh and tell me I was Dreaming, didn't advise me to Pull Myself Together and Stop Behaving like a ten year old. Instead she sat half on the desktop beside me and listened, saying little but giving comforting little nods and was impressed when I told her about the six sonnets. She said that anything was possible and didn't add Even for a Girl Like You. She warned it would mean a great deal of hard work. Twenty minutes later I adored her just a little more and felt abuzz with a new confidence knowing that I was definitely going to give Office Work a Huge Miss. I even tackled the Nile Delta in Geography after lunch with an enthusiasm that caused Miss Springate to glance at me oddly and ask if I was All

Right. Next day at lunchtime when passing the two Miss Smiths on their linked arm stroll around the park I gave them both a dazzling smile and Miss K even smiled back. My regard for her could only increase with that momentary recognition of the most important Secret I had so recently shared with her.

At this stage of my school career French was indisputably my most hated subject but it was several days before the Deluge of sadness and desperation that I have never quite forgotten would come about. It was my habit to always sit close to the corner in the second row from the back of the class and spend most of the lesson gazing over the heads of the other girls and through the tall windows of the Morning Room to the expanse of park beyond. It was also my habit to mutter an answer if called upon to respond to any question put to me in the much detested language. On the day in question at twenty minutes to three exactly Miss S Smith required a response to a query regarding buying what was needed for an imaginary picnic beside an imaginary French River in an imaginary French Town. After a few seconds of shock, I mumbled something completely inaudible.

Miss S rose from her seat at the desk at the front of the room and grew alarmingly in height. Her short black hair swung around her ears and she was unblinking as she looked at me in silence for at least fifteen seconds. Then, with the faintest glimpse of a smile, she said very clearly and precisely: "I understand you are the girl who thinks she is going to go on the stage, who in fact believes she might become a famous actress – well you're certainly going to have to work on improving your diction before that can happen, aren't you?"

The greatly despised Valerie Goldsack was the first to half cover her mouth and titter, followed by her faithful acolyte Yvonne, she who had once been my Decent Friend. The rest of them, nineteen girls in total, rapidly joined in the merriment.

Old Gravesend Hospital in Bath Street

There had been a hospital of one kind or another in Bath Street, Gravesend for more than a hundred years when I first became familiar with it. My first memory of the place was when I was four years old and had broken my arm in the park at Crayford and the park keeper chased me out at closing time along with my older cousin Margaret. He was waving a broom at the time and terrified me although Margaret claimed he was only joking. Nevertheless at the time she ran faster than I did and she was eleven and to my mind almost grown up so must have known a thing or two.

At first nobody believed that I couldn't move my right arm because even then I was inclined to hysteria and making things up just for the fun of it. However when Aunt Mag tried to tempt me with her home-made toffee – but only if I could take it with my right hand, even she began to grudgingly believe me. My mother blamed Margaret for not taking better care of me and Aunt Mag for persuading her that it was safe to let me go off for an hour in the park in the care of her oldest daughter. After all what could possibly happen to me with Margaret in charge? She was eleven when all was said and done!

On the bus ride home there was a lot of muttering about Mag not knowing her arse from her elbow where her Margaret was concerned and it was obvious there had been a sad mishap with my right arm although getting that silly cow, Mag, to admit that her Margaret was in any way to blame was like trying to push a bus uphill. The trouble with Mag was that she could never see any harm in those kids of hers even when young Harold was caught in the Co-op with half a dozen lime jellies under his jumper. It had been just the same when young Les started smoking at the age of nine. Easily led Mag had said he was, well that was a joke and a half and no mistake. It was easy to see that she would never admit that her Margaret could be to blame for what had happened in the park. My mother wished now that she'd had better sense herself and not let me go with her.

The arm had not improved the next day no matter how much Witch Hazel was rubbed onto it and that was how I found myself in Gravesend Hospital having a fracture of the shaft of the humerus reduced with the aid of a terrifying chloroform mask. Some hours later I was sent home with my right arm firmly bound to my chest where it remained for six long weeks thus ensuring that I learned to do a lot with my left arm with the help of my teeth. I was relieved that my older cousin always remained mostly responsible for the injury because secretly I wondered if there might not be repercussions for not vacating the park at the first request of the broom-waving park keeper. I had failed to admit that it was me who shouted that he was a Stinky Bum and Margaret, to give her cousinly credit, had simply said I'd been rude which my mother had chosen not to believe because after all she knew me and I was never rude to strangers apparently.

Great-great Aunt Martha from Hamerton Road, who we always called Little Nanny, came to visit and to inspect the injured arm and she said that we were very fortunate to have the Bath Road hospital and that back when she was a girl it had been known as The Infirmary.

Lord Darnley himself had given a hundred guineas to get it up and running for the Destitute Poor. Countess Darnley had opened the new children's ward in the 1880s and Little Nanny knew of many a child perishing there of the Smallpox years ago on account of no beds being available in the Fever Hospital at Springhead. Back in those days the children of the poor succumbed to disease much more often than now and those bringing up a family in the forward thinking and thoroughly modern 1940s had little idea as to how hard it had once been to raise children. True enough there was now the problem of a war and having to dodge the air raids but as for childhood illnesses we simply didn't know how lucky we now were. There had been a time when a broken arm might have been simply splinted at home between two pieces of wood and left for nature to do the rest. Little Nanny accepted a third cup of tea and warmed to her theme pointing out that Nellie herself must surely be aware of how times had changed, for instance how many of her very own little sisters had been lost before they could either walk or talk. Poor little Edith for one and little Beatrice for another, both taken by the Diphtheria in the very same week to break their poor father's heart. She did not mention baby Arthur whose untimely death had been caused by his parents lying on him in the bed when they were drunk. Neither did she comment upon the broken heart of the deceased infants' mother, Old Nan who surely must have been equally distressed. Later my mother said this omission was simply because it was my grandfather that Little Nanny was directly related to and that she had never believed the woman he chose for his wife was good enough for him.

Before she left to return to Hamerton Road, Great-great Aunt Martha's reminiscences turned back to the hospital in Bath Street. She told us that by the turn of the century there had been two new wards added, circular in design, where a nurse sat at a desk in the middle and was able to keep an eye on everything that was going on around her. They were called the Russell Wards because they had been paid for by Russells, the Brewers of Gravesend. I had never heard of Russells the Brewers but my mother seemed to know who they were. I was familiar with the philanthropic Lord Darnley because it was his woods we plundered on a regular basis with my grandmother, picking his bluebells and primroses to brighten our kitchens and collecting his chestnuts for roasting and his blackberries to add to our stewed apples.

In due time my arm healed and I had no further dealings with the Hospital until my brother had his tonsils removed there when he was two and we had to queue up to wait for the front doors to open at seven am. By that time the place had improved by leaps and bounds. A whole new wing had been added at enormous cost and later I read somewhere that the Hospital had at one stage become affiliated with the Chatham Military Hospital and during the First World War had fifty beds reserved for wounded servicemen. By 1930 when my mother and aunts had clear memories of the place, an Out Patients Department had been opened together with designated Women's Wards. By 1944, around the time I had broken my arm, it boasted more than one hundred and twenty beds. Bernard, at only two, neither knew nor cared about any of this rather predictable history but emerged from his stay wholly appreciative of the place because he had totally approved of the ice cream he had been given after his operation. It was now 1949 and our Hospital had joined the NHS under the control of the Medway and Gravesend Management Committee. There was even talk of an old Sanatorium in Whitehill Lane being converted to a maternity home. This was at a time when the majority of women had their babies at home unless they were what my mother described as Toffee Nosed with more money than sense.

The hospital was a thriving, busy place by mid-December 1951 when my father was to die there quite out of the blue and unexpectedly. It boasted one hundred and fifty beds and he occupied one for just two or three days. The average weekly cost of supporting an in-patient had soared and the average length of stay for most was three weeks. Everyone agreed that the advent of the NHS meant that we didn't know how lucky we were as far as accessing medical assistance was concerned. This had not been the case for him of course.

My last direct contact with the Hospital was in the early winter of 1952 when I had been left in charge of my young brother whilst my mother worked extra hours for the Lovells, helping them prepare for Christmas because they were about to entertain relatives from Brighton. Bernard was now growing taller, wanting to be treated like a Real Boy instead of a baby being now five and a half years old. He had no intention of staying inside the house with me playing the kind of games I insisted on which involved him dressing up as a girl called Wendy. He preferred to retreat outside to The Old Green with Hedley Davis who was also being allowed to be a Proper Grown Up Boy. I agreed, just as long as he was back by the time our mother returned just after five, and buried myself in my latest Monica Edwards library book. He returned only an hour or so later with a horrifying looking leg injury which involved a large segment of skin rolled back and flapping against his shin. There was also rather more blood than I was comfortable with.

I reluctantly reached the conclusion that this situation could only be improved by enlisting the services of the hospital as the local doctor's surgery was not due to open until early evening. The whole venture was complicated by the fact that a thick fog was now descending upon Northfleet but at twelve years of age I paid little heed to this because my main motivation was ensuring that the injury should look a great deal tidier by the time my mother returned. Tidying it up I reasoned would result in me being in less trouble for causing it in the first place. Pulling a long school sock and a handkerchief over the offending flap of wayward skin I pulled him by the hand along Springhead Road where a man was in the throes of abandoning the cleaning of his small, shiny, black car. As we had no bus fare I decided to beg a lift to the hospital telling myself that the worst that could happen was that he said No. To my surprise after a minute or two of doubt and a whispered conversation with his wife in which I could tell she was very negative, he did not say No – he said Yes. We hopped into the back of the little black car and the Good Samaritan drove slowly and carefully through the deepening gloom and let us out in Bath Street, wishing us luck.

There was a long wait before my brother's leg was stitched and bandaged and an interrogation as to how we came to be so totally unsupervised which I was not prepared for as those were days when children were much less observed, organised and regulated than they are today, particularly children from working class homes. However, I found myself concocting a colourful story which involved my mother having to meet a fictitious relative from an airport. It did not in my innocence regarding air travel, occur to me that all planes might be grounded along with the local buses all of which appeared to be coming to a grinding halt. It took a very long time to reach home again because the pea-souper that had descended was of astonishing proportions and we had to grope our way along the London Road very cautiously indeed.

Later it was called The Great Smog of 1952 and was caused by air pollution combined with an anticyclone and totally windless conditions. Over several days it was so persistent that it penetrated the very houses and thousands of people died as a direct result of it. That fateful afternoon our mother was also detained by the dreadful conditions and so fortunately we arrived back in York Road a few minutes before she did and we were only reprimanded for allowing the fire to go out during such weather. I don't think she really knew what to say about the hospital visit and seemed grudgingly approving of me hijacking a lift from one of the Springhead Road neighbours because we all knew they were full of their own importance, particularly the few car owners among them.

When Old Nan came visiting a day or two later she reported that the fog had played Merry Hell with her bronchitis and her coughing had had to be heard to be believed. She also said it put her in mind of Bethnal Green in the old days when she was a girl and Jack the Ripper had roamed the streets. It was well known, she said, that nothing pleased him more than a good pea-souper.

As for Gravesend Hospital, I had nothing further to do with the place whatsoever although I was told in the early 1970s that a new wing had opened with fifty beds and a Special Care Baby Unit. A few years ago I was astonished to find that I barely recognized the environs in which it now stands and it had become Gravesham Community Hospital.

Wash Day

There was once a definite ritual around what was generally accomplished on the various days of the week, quite unlike nowadays. Monday was, without fail, always Wash Day even when it was raining – not just for us but for everyone around us as well. It wasn't easy to opt out of Wash Day even if you wanted to, and not many would have wanted to. Even if the bedsheets were only changed on a fortnightly basis, and not many housewives would have admitted to such a housekeeping slip-up, it remained a fact that a family needed two changes of underclothing per person, per week. A regular wash day, therefore, was essential.

Along with the rest of England, Northfleet housewives were expected to wash on Monday and the neighbours might even enter into gossip if that didn't happen. My mother would have definitely considered anyone avoiding the expectations of Monday to be slovenly which was a word she took to using a good deal. She might have described such a miscreant as slummocky, which had more of a ring to it and definitely conjured up the right picture in the mind's eye. Either way, Wash Day was never missed in our house at least not as far as I can recall. And it started early both summer and winter before six with a fire lit under the scullery copper for the basic and necessary heating of water. Whites were churned vigorously in the copper: sheets, pillow cases and anything made from cotton. Little by little the modest terraced houses began to fill with the steam that would only begin to diminish by Thursday.

Each terraced dwelling had a copper in the scullery, every one brick-built with a small fireplace beneath and each came supplied with a wooden lid and a sturdy copper stick to aid the twenty minutes or so of churning. When I was small I was warned to keep well away from the copper when it was in use because it was considered a hazardous space. Dark stories were told of children who did not heed such warnings and reaped the terrible consequences. The only one I remember was the cautionary tale of the four-year-old boy who, when dismounting his tricycle, managed to lower his leg into the boiling water and thereafter walked with a limp. His name was Brian and I was told he had very nearly died of shock and so, for different reasons, did his long suffering mother who had given him many a warning so when all was said and done, it wasn't her fault poor soul; he should have listened.

While the whites were agitating, pans of water would be heated on top of the gas cooker for the dolly tub to be filled and the remainder of the wash to begin. Nightdresses, knickers, shirts and socks would now be rubbed against the washboard with the aid of Sunlight soap, bright yellow and looking fit for the job. My mother attired in a print overall, her hair covered in a bright checked scarf, sweat pouring down her face, would pause from time to time to sip from an enamel mug of tea. I would be sitting like a Good Girl on the scullery step and if the day was cold and the door to the backyard was closed, a great deal of the washday steam would have magically transformed itself into water that ran liberally over the walls but the scullery itself would be oddly, snugly, tropically balmy. So memorable was this Monday morning ambiance that on my first visit to Singapore decades later I was instantly, sharply reminded of York Road washdays past.

With luck on our side the arduous task of rinsing the soap from the piles of washing could begin by eight am when the Reckitt's Blue Bag was added to the final rinsing water. It was a long time before I realized that the object of the Blue Bag was to make Whites appear as white as humanly possible before they were manhandled, piece by piece, into the terrifying jaws of the mangle. Our mangle, huge and made of wrought iron with wooden rollers, lived just outside the back door against the wall of the lavatory. In fact you had to pass it on every lavatory visit you made and it could be strangely comforting to bump into its solid hulk on moonless winter nights but on Wash Day it became a disturbing beast. It was a slightly complicated piece of technology in that the space between the rollers could be adjusted if you knew how. Nobody in our family had ever been initiated into the mysteries of fine-tuning its performance and I was constantly reminded of unfortunate children like Brian whose fate has already been detailed, wayward children whose fingers had been wrenched from their hands or flattened beyond recognition on account of foolish meddling with mangles. I lived in fear of joining their ranks and though I was a curious and often disobedient child, I curbed my enthusiasm for exploration of mangles.

By noon, with a degree of sunshine and a modicum of luck the week's wash would be tidily pegged to the line with pegs made by my grandmother from slim offcuts of willow that between washes I was allowed to play with as long as I put them all back in the peg basket when I had finished. As I grew a little older and was persuaded by my father to attempt to read difficult books like *Little Women* I learned that Meg March had used a clothes peg nightly pinned to her nose in order to improve its shape. I found it strangely painful when I tried it myself and abandoned the idea when there was no perceptible change in shape on the third morning. Mostly I did not experiment much with the pegs and they were usually merely students in my School for Pegs or patients in my Hospital for Pegs. Later, as my brother grew older they at times became soldiers defending Kent from Roman invaders. We were not possessed of many toys.

Usually on Mondays, unless the day had been excellent for drying, we ate our tea of toast and dripping amidst still damp sheets and shirts hung from cords that criss-crossed the kitchen and forced us to duck and dive in order to avoid them. By morning with a degree of luck the Monday wash would be ready for ironing and by the time I was seven years old our family had become the very proud owners of an electric iron. As far as I can remember this enviable and convenient aid to modern housekeeping was proudly purchased from Frost's in Northfleet High Street by my father to mark the birth of my baby brother in April 1947. It was definitely a step up from the flat irons of my earlier childhood. Nevertheless, rather inconveniently it had to be plugged into the light socket above the kitchen table which entailed mounting a chair and first removing the light bulb. This in turn meant that ironing could only take place in daylight hours and so it usually took place on

Tuesday mornings. It was a hazardous process and sturdy shoes needed to be worn because somehow or other my mother had come to believe that shoes would protect her from death by electrocution. My cousin Margaret, ironing a school blouse, was once thrown across the kitchen in Iron Mill Lane, Crayford simply because her feet were clad only in cotton socks. She could very well have been killed, at least that is what I was told and from that moment on, I also had a healthy respect for electric irons and to this day I sometimes wonder if I should change my footwear before beginning the task.

Even though by Tuesday evening the week's ironing was completed, the regular washday ritual was not totally concluded because the sheets and shirts still had to be aired and so they once again hung above us on the improvised indoor lines until they were safe to use. My mother believed that the consequences of wearing a damp liberty bodice would be dire and pneumonia would most likely result. Thankfully I have not inherited this particular conviction and my own children happily donned damp garments without noticeable health problems throughout their childhood.

In the 1940s, Wash Day and its aftermath was an exhaustive undertaking and considering this it was not entirely unreasonable that our clean clothes were rationed. Until I reached the age of not quite sixteen and was about to leave school I was never allocated more than two clean pairs of knickers and socks weekly and it simply did not occur to me to protest. One pink floral winceyette nightdress was donned after each Saturday evening bath and not discarded until the following

Saturday and when I grew older and attended Colyer Road Secondary School and Wombwell Hall, I was granted just one clean blouse weekly. This latter garment was decidedly grimy and slightly smelly by Thursday each week which was understandable as not much mid-week washing of necks and underarms took place. On the other hand back then most of us smelt the same, even those boasting brand new bathrooms on spanking new housing estates, because old habits died hard as far as general cleanliness was concerned, at least that's how it was then. And if this appears just a little distasteful from a modern viewpoint it helps to consider that a hundred years earlier the situation would have been even more dire and two or three hundred years ago simply doesn't bear thinking about.

In 1952 at Colyer Road Secondary School during a history lesson that these days would more likely be called Social Studies, the enthusiastic young Supply Teacher urged us to speak with our grandparents about how life had changed over decades, ask our grandmothers what household tasks had been like when they were young mothers. I wasn't all that keen so rather half-heartedly enquired of Old Nan what her own Wash Day had been like in those years before the first World War when she already had half a dozen small children. She said it had been not much trouble to her on account of The Bagwash. I never found out exactly what The Bagwash entailed and lacked the confidence to enquire how many clean underclothes she doled out weekly to her brood. I strongly suspected changes of clothing were few and far between.

There's no doubt at all that the emergence of modern washing facilities in the form of modern bathrooms and automatic washing machines and dryers in every home has transformed the ease with which we can now monitor bodily odours and how many clean pairs of knickers we allow ourselves each week.

Brian Philpott.

I had not given Brian Philpott a thought for years, not until a neighbour recently spoke of her young brother, born with Down Syndrome. We discussed the need for inclusion and how over decades society's attitude toward children with disabilities has inexorably changed for the better. Later I found myself thinking about Brian and wondering about our attitudes toward him as he grew up in Shepherd Street. Did we always include him in our games and how did he feel on the occasions when he wasn't allowed to play? But back then any one of us might be embraced into an activity, or not, almost upon the whim of he who had suggested the game in the first place. Can Anybody Play? was the oft repeated catchphrase from those merging on the fringes of the game, half question, half merely ritual expectation of immediate inclusion. Did Brian understand this customary question? Was he ever turned down?

Back then we knew nothing of chromosome abnormalities and had of course never heard of John Langden Down who apparently had first described the condition in 1862. Because of the features of the affected children he called them Mongoloid and in 1949, some ninety years later so did we. My mother said Brian was a Poor Little Bugger and wouldn't live long because children like him never did and that all them Mongols were slow. It wasn't until 1961, long after I had left the district and pushed all memory of him from my consciousness that scientists began to suggest that the term Mongolism had misleading connotations and had become an embarrassing term. It was dropped completely in 1965 and those with a connection to children with the condition had to learn overnight to describe them as having Down Syndrome. To be fair it probably wasn't nearly as hard for those with an afflicted family member as it was for the rest of us. Most of us, with the exception of course of the medical profession and those training to be social workers, continued to describe children like Brian as Mongols. This meant that we were treated to hostile and superior looks or as time went on, the error of our terminology was pointed out to us.

But when we were children it was still perfectly acceptable for Brian to be referred to as a Mongol. He was supremely unaware of all this and a more cheerful and chirpy child would have been hard to find. He lived at number 60 Shepherd Street with Annie and Albert Philpott who were his parents although for many years I thought they were his grandparents. This error was partly because Old Nan, who thought she knew everything, maintained that his mother had Scarpered and after all, who could blame her? My grandmother was well known for jumping to conclusions and as my mother was wont to point out, getting the wrong end of the stick.

What Brian may have lacked in intelligence he made up for in enthusiasm and was always more than anxious to join in any group game being played and happy to take on roles that the rest of us discarded on account of them being monotonous. Brian never tired of the tedious and the repetitive and was simply delighted to be accepted as part of the crowd, guarding camps, searching for lost balls and inexpertly keeping scores without argument and with a cheerful countenance. He loved being with each and every one of us and did not seem to attempt to analyse why it was that although he was usually willingly included in group activities, singly it was harder for him to find a playmate, especially among the boys. The only one of us always agreeable to playing with Brian on a one to one basis was Kathleen Draper who lived a few doors away from him. He called her My Kath and loved her dearly, following a step or two behind her and obeying her every instruction. And Kathleen looked after him like a mother although she was only a year or so his senior, ensuring that from time to time he got Proper Turns in games and prepared to put up a fight on his behalf if anyone argued about it. Even in more complex pastimes like What's The Time Mr Wolf when nobody ever really wanted Brian to be the wolf, Kathleen would take his hand when he got muddled and tirelessly explain that it couldn't always be Time to Eat you Up which was his favourite part of the procedure. And with her beside him, holding on to him tightly, he rose to the occasion and managed to remember for a moment or two.

I can't recall Brian going to school with us so perhaps he went to a special class somewhere in the neighbourhood along with Elsie Coppins from Buckingham Road who was in a wheelchair because she couldn't walk, or maybe he wasn't required to attend at all. My mother said there was no point anyway because if you were like him you'd never learn to read and write because you simply wouldn't have what it took. It stood to reason and it was his poor grandmother she felt sorry for. Nevertheless Kathleen was making firm attempts to teach Brian to read and he could already recognize B for

Brian and K for Kath. She said she didn't mind how long it took because it had to be done. This was because Brian wanted to be a train driver and he would need to be able to read at the very least the names of the local stations. Even as a ten-year-old I understood why he loved her so devotedly.

The Passng of Greta Thilthorpe

There are definitely positive aspects to having an online social media account, although at times I agree that the negative aspects can be weighty. Without it I would never have heard of the recent passing of Greta Thilthorpe, that erstwhile best friend of my early teenage years. It was Dawn who told me, a friend I have never actually met but I feel as if I know because that's the way things are with social media.

Greta was the remarkably sensible Only Girl in a large family featuring a clutch of moodily handsome boys and a rather exotic mother with a penchant for red chiffon and heavy jewellery. Well so it seemed to me at the time but then you have to bear in mind that when I first became Greta's friend I had only very recently celebrated my thirteenth birthday. She on the other hand was seventeen and in her final year at Wombwell Hall just as I was about to start my first. I think our slightly unusual friendship came about in the first place because my mother had just started to work for The Trokes at their shop in Shepherd Street where Greta's mother had been employed for several years. I was to inherit Greta's outgrown school uniforms although I was already in possession of those of my cousin Connie. This undoubtedly saved my mother a significant sum of money but as both girls were of a more slender build than myself I was destined for the duration of my time at the school to wear uncomfortably tight clothing. I was fast becoming what my Uncle Harold described as a fine specimen of English Womanhood and what Young Harold, his elder son, described as Fat. My mother claimed that I was not fat at all, but merely stout. I could not decide which of the trio I hated most. In any event, as we certainly did not have money to burn on trivialities like new school uniforms that actually fitted, I was required to wear the cast off skirts and blouses of others whether I liked the idea or not.

I gladly became Greta's friend though being several years my senior my mother did rather wonder if it was a good idea. The one thing she did not want was me being corrupted by an older girl because a few months before Greta came into my life I had become friendly with yet another seventeen-year-old, this time one called Shirley who worked for Ripleys the greengrocers. Shirley had permed hair and pierced ears and a boyfriend who was doing his National Service. She introduced me to cigarettes and gin and staying out late and so a halt was called to the friendship quite rapidly. I learned that Shirley had been Fast and that was something you certainly couldn't accuse Greta of. She was, however, canny and had a knack of saying rude things to older women such as Peggy Troke, with a guileless expression in both voice and face that led them to believe she was just being refreshingly frank.

She was also exceptionally generous and my cousin Connie who was not especially known for her own generosity said that was simply because only daughters in families of boys were brought up to share whether they liked it or not. Both Connie and Greta had been blessed with a multitude of brothers though Connie's were noisy and smelly and largely of no interest to me which is generally how one feels when the boys in question are cousins. Greta's were quiet and polite and as far as I recall did not smell. Of them all I remember Michael best because he was fifteen years old and dazzlingly handsome so I spent some time attempting to gain his attention. This was fruitless and for his part he failed completely to notice me even when I wore Evening in Paris perfume to his parent's twenty-fifth wedding anniversary.

Greta was not only a highly intelligent girl who did exceptionally well academically and although I think she had enrolled in the Commercial Course at Wombwell Hall rather than the Domestic, she had firm ambitions for her future that did not involve joining a typing pool. She told me that she was going to go into teaching and in fact would be very keen at some future stage to run her own school. Ideally it would be an establishment catering to the educational needs of five- to eleven-year-olds where those attending would not be required to become involved in activities that did not appeal to them, like team games. She was not overly enthralled with team games, an attitude I wholeheartedly supported. When I asked if she would apply those same attitudes to topics like Mathematics she hesitated and said her pupils would be gently persuaded to develop a liking for mathematics but there would be no coercion. This ideal school would hopefully be situated in a local village and she was confident that when the time came she would be able to find the perfect property.

She also had an extraordinarily well developed work ethic. During the years of our friendship Greta seemed easily able to locate all the local farms that largely and quite illegally employed child labour for harvesting work. This was work that adults in the district were beginning to avoid because it paid what my grandmother said was a pittance. Greta was unconcerned with pay rates and simply lined us both up for work that usually began at five am each morning of the school holidays. This meant that unlike many of our peers she and I had, for a time at least, money to spend on sweets, ice creams, Smith's crisps and bottles of Tizer. Even my ever critical grandmother admitted that Greta was a Grafter and no mistake!

In addition to all these virtues she was also something of an adventurer and that was an attitude that greatly appealed to me at the time. Although I was quite unable to persuade Molly Freeman to embark upon a train trip in the general direction of London and when I suggested the idea to Joan Bennett she simply looked dazed and said she'd have to ask her Mum, it did not occur to Greta that mothers should ever be asked permission to do something as ordinary as boarding a train. Mothers were busy people she said, and had more on their minds than train trips. She had a system of getting to London without ever paying a proper fare, simply by purchasing a platform ticket. In fact on two occasions we got as far as London Bridge when Greta began to doubt the practicalities of the plan and deftly led us to the correct platform for our return to Gravesend where we handed in our platform tickets to the uninterested collector with smiles and thank yous. In the same manner over a month or two we embarked upon similar outings to Maidstone, Gillingham and even Whitstable. These were adventures unfamiliar to most of my Wombwell Hall classmates and so because of the daring of Greta Thilthorpe I gained a certain amount of kudos among the girls of 1SC that year. Sadly I failed completely to make any impression whatsoever upon her highly desirable brother Michael.

Local Pubs & Links With History

Unlike many of our neighbours, my parents did not drink alcohol to any great extent and their visits to local pubs were almost entirely driven by other concerns. In the first place the pub on the corner provided a common and generally safe venue for day to day socialising with neighbours where conversation could take place on subjects of mutual interest. In the second place this socialising need only cost the price of a couple of half pints of Mild & Bitter if pay day was several days away. You certainly did not have to have a fondness for large quantities of alcohol to frequent the local pub. On the other hand, of course, there were those attendees whose affection for strong liquor was certainly to the general detriment of their families.

Northfleet, like all similar small towns made up largely of the labouring classes, provided plenty of Public Houses to choose from, many of which my parents chose never to enter. After we had grown up and left the immediate area my brother and I determined to try each of those that remained mostly unfamiliar to us in an attempt to better know that region in which we had spent our formative years. We learned that The Black Eagle in Galley Hill Road first opened in 1866 but it had definitely closed by the end of 1968 when we decided to visit one evening. A little disheartened, because there is nothing more disheartening than a pub that is definitely closed, ultimately we ended up in the nearby Ingress Tavern which luckily had stood the test of time. I had vague recollections of both places from our childhood when on summer evenings my parents once or twice visited on my father's motorbike, me and Bernard in the side-car. I certainly hadn't given either much thought in the intervening years though which is perhaps not surprising as each was somewhat devoid of character. Many pubs of that vintage are apt to be so no matter how much we choose to eulogise them later. The nearby Plough in Stonebridge Road was of a similar vintage and was where a boy in my brother's class at St Joseph's had celebrated his twenty-first birthday and invited all of his former schoolmates. It was to undergo several rapid changes as we hurtled towards the millennium, unnerving those patrons who knew it well. Then a decade on in 2010 it became The Cosmopolitan but was The Golden Grill by 2012. Perhaps predictably, despite our complaints of drinking venues being dull and dreary none of us are ever terribly enthusiastic about those we remember from a shared past daring to change too radically.

My classmate from St Botolph's School, Margaret Snelling, had an aged aunt who lived in Stonebridge Road and said she clearly recalled The Plough at the beginning of the First War, as a place where a group of local lads met up for pints to send them on their way to The Front. They all looked so handsome and so brave, she told us. Yet sadly despite that courage not all of them had survived – the likes of young Freddie Holt and Arthur Deadman for instance and she could, she said, name at least a dozen more if she had all her wits about her but at her age memory was fading. She'd only been a slip of a girl herself back then and helped out in the bar at weekends when called upon to do so.

Another nearby Northfleet hostelry much favoured by some of our aunts was The Railway Tavern at 69 The High Street that had opened in 1858 and met its demise in 1967 along with a number of similar establishments. Little Nanny from Hamerton Road had always found it an acceptable place to visit for half a pint of Milk Stout. She said it had in general been a more genteel place than most. She could never be persuaded to enter The Edinburgh Castle also in The High Street or The Rose in Wood Street, both of which were still thriving only a few years ago. Old Nan was once was reputed to have descended upon The Edinburgh Castle dressed in her best intent upon just one drink before proceeding onward for an afternoon at Rosherville Gardens, then famous for a variety of entertainments. Unfortunately on this occasion she made the fatal decision to have a second then a third drink and even missed the last train back to Crayford. This, she always felt was a pity, since she had been Dolled Up To The Nines and even sported a brand new hat with an ostrich feather.

I don't remember much about The Huggens Arms at 10 The Creek which opened in 1860 and apparently changed its name in the 1960s. I recall visiting the place only once in 1955 as a teenager and feeling very nervous. I had dared my then boyfriend to take us there and order us both gin and orange. Although he was barely sixteen we were served without incident despite looking strangely out of place among the half dozen or so elderly men leaning over the bar who only seemed mildly unsettled by our bursts of giggling. Later I learned that it was said to have been one of my father's favourite places to pop inside from time to time with his latest Bit on the Side on his arm.

The New Blue Anchor at 5 The Creek that closed as long ago as 1908 was definitely spoken of by my grandmother who claimed to have pulled her Edgar out of the place more than once and furthermore said that it was a dead and alive hole and not worth the effort of stepping over the doorstep. Its only family significance was that apparently it closed in the year my mother was born in the hop gardens at Mereworth. Locally it was known that Old Lil who at that time delivered babies and laid out the dead, lived nearby and was in the place twice a week as Regular as Clockwork should anyone wish to converse with her.

Pubs more familiar to us as we grew up in York Road, Northfleet were those that were not in fact Destinations but rather places to be dropped into from time to time when passing, thus almost becoming an extension of home. In those days when the Wireless was the only form of home entertainment, casual pub visiting was undoubtedly more customary than it is today and definitely a more accessible pastime than Going to the Pictures. People definitely had their favourites and a place that was spoken fondly of by one very elderly neighbour was The Dove which had been on The Hill adjacent to the lychgate of St Botolph's Church, and sadly burnt down in the early years of the twentieth century, presumably making way for the Infants' Playground of St Botolph's School. As a small child old Mrs Beresford had lingered in the doorway frequently, observing her parents consuming quantities of gin. If she complained she was given a drop of gin and water and sometimes fell asleep outside. At other times she said, a complaint might simply result in a clip around the ear. On one momentous occasion she had been completely forgotten about and woke up to find everything still and quiet and had to run home and let herself in the scullery window. She was fearful that it might turn out to be her fault and result in a beating but luckily it didn't.

Whilst some places come and go and change their names and eventually accommodate Thai restaurants, others for some reason endure without too many changes. A year or two ago, I was cheered to find that The Coach & Horses at 25 The Hill, was still open and serving a hearty Sunday lunch. It had remained a remarkably atmospheric place with many of the original features still intact. The proprietor told us that it was said to date back to the mid-1700s when it had been called The Three Horseshoes. It had been one of my brother's favourite Inns back in the early 1960s when he proudly introduced me to his first girlfriend Christine, the girl he was going to love forever. They were both sixteen and lost within an intensely passionate relationship. To Bernard The Coach & Horses was simply the smartest place he knew locally and therefore fitting as a place in which to entertain his Beloved together with his sister and so we sat beneath its ancient beams sipping slowly on our vodka, nibbling Smith's Crisps and trying desperately hard to look stylish. When I revisited the place more recently I was impressed both with the way it had stood the test of time with little visible deterioration in its antiquity, and also offering a Sunday lunch which was both substantial and delicious.

Happily, in recent years I came to rediscover The Leather Bottel at 1 Dover Road dating from 1706 and opportunely it was also still open for business. However, the inside of the building has been so modernised and upgraded as to be all but destroyed from a historical perspective and completely belies the still enticing promise of the exterior. This was at one stage my mother's favourite Local if one of her sisters should suggest a Milk Stout or Half of Mild and a Sunday afternoon gossip. It appears to have been a coaching inn at one time and according to historical accounts it provided excellent stabling. As the adjacent road into Gravesend was said to have been dangerous at the time, presumably eroded by the incessant digging for chalk, rather than the presence of Highwaymen, it is possible that The Leather Bottel was a convenient place for many travellers in which to take pause and consider the best way to progress forward. Back in the early days of the 20th century Little Nanny had been friendly with Martha Johnson, the mother of the then proprietor and told us that coming from Dublin Martha had found Northfleet a difficult place to settle into, one of the reasons being that she believed The Leather Bottel to be haunted. My mother always maintained she wouldn't have relished being in the building alone because it certainly was haunted by not just one, but two different lost souls and that was why she always needed company to visit the upstairs Ladies convenience. A former maid who died under questionable circumstances was usually only observed on the upper floor but downstairs a tall dark man was frequently seen and was said to have committed suicide. At one time the place was the venue for holding inquests into the deaths of those born in the parish and if I had known all this when I was patiently waiting for my mother and aunts outside the building in 1948, devoid of entertainment, I might not have squabbled quite so much with my cousin Pat, who was a more patient waiter than me!

Those pubs closest to us we always treated with disdain and in fact my mother who said that you wouldn't catch her walking into them even if she was dying of thirst. They were determinedly lively places with nothing genteel about them and no designated corners for ladies to sit that might attract potential patrons such as Little Nanny. The Prince Albert at 62 Shepherd Street was almost on the corner of York Road and had opened in 1855. This pub closed a few years ago and has now been converted to a pre-school but before this happened I was able to visit one summer afternoon and sit drinking cider in the recently established tiny courtyard. A little later I took photos of both the front and rear of the place and the bar staff then took photographs of me simply because they thought it decidedly odd that a stranger should seem to be so preoccupied with a backstreet bar.

The British Volunteer was in Buckingham Road and quite the rowdiest and most popular place in the neighbourhood on Friday and Saturday nights. It opened in 1889 and was demolished in the 1960s to make way for the building of flats. But in the late 1940s it was very much still open for business and my mother's one time best friend, Grace Bennett, whose husband frequented the Public Bar, regularly told us that it was there her Frank happened to hear that the local council in their stupidity were about to create rose beds and flower gardens in the New House Farm housing estate and what a waste of money it would be. Frank also heard that The Battle of Britain at Shears Green was shortly to open as a Charrington House and suggested he and Grace might pay a visit at the earliest opportunity. Despite the interesting gossip, some of which was more salacious and could not be repeated, my mother could still not be persuaded to patronise The Volly. Even without her patronage, however, it went from strength to strength and at times, especially on warm summer evenings, was so crowded that the patrons spilled out onto the pavement and into the very road itself. The British Volunteer not only went in for Darts matches and illegal betting but also regular sing-songs to keep their decidedly working class clientele happy and the local children for miles around, awake. In its heyday it was undoubtedly the most popular pub in the area.

In the late 1940s one of our occasional Sunday afternoon destinations was The Fleet Tavern in Waterdales. It was a thoroughly modern and up to date place, having opened in 1938 and it had a Children's Room for the use of those with baby-sitting problems or the kind of offspring it would not be safe to leave home alone. We went there to meet up with my Uncle Walter, who was my father's older brother and lived in Waterdales. Sometimes he would bring his wife and two or three of his many children. If that happened, my father would disappear into the Public Bar with him and the rest of us would remain in the Children's Room. It was all a bit boring once we got over the initial excitement of being given lemonade, sometimes with ice, and a packet of crisps. I solved this by initiating fights with my cousin Georgie who was only there because he was one of those children it was not safe to leave at home. This always worried his sister Connie who was a year older than me and a very responsible child; possibly she knew that in the end it would definitely be her fault for not managing the situation properly. Uncle Walter was a very hard taskmaster and I was definitely frightened of him but he had an impressive intellect coupled with some very old-fashioned ideas. It was he who informed my father during the late 1940s that Wombwell Hall had just been purchased by the Kent Education Committee and would shortly be turned into the kind of girls' school where those like me and his Connie might be taught a number of housewifely skills that would prove invaluable in years to come.

The slightly more distant Battle of Britain pub increasingly became a weekend destination for families like ours in those years that followed World War Two and the stories concerning how many brave young pilots had made the place their own abounded and the undoubted truth regarding the place became intermingled with a great deal of undoubted fiction. Gravesend air base had become a satellite airfield for Biggin Hill in the early stages of the war under the control of No 11 Group Fighter Command. During the Battle itself the Hurricanes from No 501 Squadron were primarily using Gravesend. As an eight-year-old I found it exciting to go there though I was uncomprehending of the history of the place. More interesting to me were the piles of comics and Rupert Bear Annuals on hand for the amusement of young visitors. There was also play equipment in the garden in the form of swings and a slide. This forward thinking attitude of the landlord ensured that the place was constantly busy at weekends.

I had a poignant reminder of the place a few years back when listening to late night radio in New Zealand. I was enormously cheered when the Midnight to Dawn host, a well-known Maori broadcaster who had just come back from his first visit to England, began to talk about his trip. He said the highlight had been going to a place called Gravesend in North Kent, twenty miles or so from London. He went there he said, not because he had any connections whatsoever with the district, but because he wanted to visit one of the places where the only battle that was ever fought and won in the air, had to a great extent taken place. Since his school days he had developed a yearning to stand in the nearby fields and look up into the very sky in which it had all happened and cogitate upon those dramatic events of WW2. And then he was thrilled to be able to go into the local pub, aptly called The Battle of Britain, a place those young pilots would have undoubtedly been familiar with. He drank a pint of beer and was glad that the pub existed and had been preserved for the memory of that critical point in history!

And I was glad too – glad that an important link to those historical events remained at least as a place where someone from across the globe and completely disconnected, but with a yen to uncover a splinter of modern history could sit and muse and sample English beer. It is therefore difficult to make any sensible comment on the fact that the place has since been demolished.

Of Cleaning & Cats

Despite the fact that we never had very much that absolutely needed to be kept clean, a lot of cleaning of one kind or another seemed to go on at our house. The kind of cleaning that doesn't happen much these days. I remember a dark red polish with a picture of a funny looking man on the screw top, who called himself Cardinal and not having much of a clue about the hierarchy of the Church at the time I believed him to be the person who made the polish or was at least in charge of the process. I thought it was rather avant-garde of him to have his picture on every tin.

On Tuesday mornings unless it was raining the front door step was spruced up with the help of Cardinal, followed by the flagstones in front of the kitchen stove. I was never allowed to help with these jobs although I was keen to do so, finding the smell of the gloopy red stuff almost intoxicating. I envied Jennifer Berryman whose grandmother always allowed her to polish their front step though it took her half the morning and even I could see that she used rather too much Cardinal and even then didn't achieve much of a shine. I was told that Jennifer was only given the job to save her grandmother's back because at her age to bend gave her gyp. It was a fact that the regular application of Cardinal to front steps was a matter of principle as far as most of the local housewives were concerned and those who avoided the task were thought to be slovenly.

Another time consuming and regular job for the woman whose work was never done was the black leading of the kitchen stove. I'm not sure that this was carried out on a weekly basis because it was a mission for which my mother covered her hair and clothes with her oldest scarf and overall and at times even wore yellow rubber gloves before carefully removing the lid from the Zebo Blacking. I most definitely was not allowed to take part, and probably neither was Jennifer no matter how bad her grandmother's back happened to be, but I could certainly watch the proceedings from a safe distance and bring fresh newspaper when asked. When I was little, long before I got what my cousin Margaret called highfaluting ideas about my own importance, I thought our stove was one of the best things about our house. This was way back before I began to long for an indoor lavatory, preferably situated inside an indoor bathroom. Back then I loved coming home to the warmth and security of the freshly black-leaded stove in winter when my mother might make toast on a long toasting fork for tea or bake potatoes in their jackets in the oven. The more modern gas stove in the scullery did not ever have quite the same appeal whatever might be cooked upon it or in it. In winter the kitchen stove was without doubt the most cost effective way to cook despite the heat being at times variable. Slow cooked vegetable stews enriched with the odd bit of bacon could simmer on the hob for hours and fill the house with a smell that promised a tasty supper and there was no anxiety that the gas might suddenly Go Out and have to be replenished with pennies in the meter. In those days at our end of the street we still had gas light because electricity had not quite reached us before the war interrupted the modernising process. The lights going out never caused much drama as far as I was concerned as long as a fire still burned in the grate and in any event we seemed to always be able to find a candle. Later on when we boasted an electricity meter alongside the gas meter in the coal cupboard under the stairs, not only did it have to be fed with shillings rather than pennies, but when it suddenly went out it caused an instant shock. My friend Pearl said years later when sitting in the Banfield's front room courting with her boyfriend, that she lived in fear of the embarrassment of the lights going out. It simply did not happen, she maintained, at his house and she wondered how she could be expected to live down the humiliation of the family scrabbling around and calling one to another for an elusive shilling piece.

At some stage in the early 1950s we joined the neighbourhood trend and rid ourselves of the old fashioned cast iron stove that needed to be pampered with Zebo on a regular basis. It was replaced with what was described as a Modern Tiled Surround which turned out to be an open fireplace edged with anaemic looking pale pink tiles. My mother was very keen to make this transition once the Bennetts of Buckingham Road installed one and Grace Bennett had extolled its many virtues over several cups of tea a day or two later, maintaining that it had been worth every penny. Her daughter Joan whispered to me that she couldn't say she agreed at all because the one thing it wasn't was cosy and for her part she greatly appreciated the cosiness of its predecessor. She added that it was impossible to make proper toast with a tiled surround. Her mother said she didn't need to make toast on a fork anymore because they now owned an electric toaster and Joan said it didn't taste the same. Later my mother pointed out that Joan Bennett was still being Spoilt Rotten. You could tell by the way she wouldn't stop whining on and on about toast not to mention the way she demanded to have her weekly bath in the kitchen rather than the scullery just so she could watch their new TV set at the same time. Privately I agreed with Joan but I didn't say so because I could see there was no stopping a tiled surround invading our kitchen.

    I was right and within a week the change had been organised with Porter, Putt & Fletcher in Gravesend and our cast iron stove was wrenched from the place where it had sat for more than a hundred years and deposited at the end of the garden awaiting the scrap metal merchant. In no time at all we were sporting a tiled surround and were never again to make proper toast or jacket potatoes or simmer soups for hours in winter time.

    A word or two should be mentioned regarding the regular cleaning job that seemed, and undoubtedly was, quite a reckless undertaking in those years after the war. The cleaning of upper floor windows was not for the faint hearted but despite the risk involved every house proud woman was able to balance precariously on the narrow window sills whilst vigorously applying pink viscous Windolene to panes of glass with scrunched up sheets of newspaper. Strangely I was never fearful that my mother was going to fall into the street below, simply because no-one ever did and quite apart from that I saw her as potently powerful where cleaning was concerned. The cleanliness of windows was just as significant as applying Cardinal to a front door step – almost a duty to the community. Only your nearest and dearest were likely to observe how often Zebo had been used on the kitchen stove simply because only relatives and close friends were invited to step inside houses but every passer-by could see the state of windows and door steps. For that reason when new curtains were made, the patterned side was invariably hung to face the street so all and sundry could witness that the front room at your place had been freshly adorned and no expense had been spared. At least, that was the idea. Meanwhile those who sat inside the room experienced the back side of the new drapes. This probably didn't matter nearly as much as might be imagined as we very rarely sat in our front room, using it only at Christmas or when very special visitors came calling.

Our lavatory was cleaned every week with Lavvo which I was told ensured it was spotless. It was attacked briskly with an ancient lavatory brush and my mother was not at all averse to pushing her hand around the S bend as far as it would go because what she could not abide was a filthy lavvy. Her older sister Mag diminished considerably in her estimation when she let that lovely new lavvy in that lovely new bathroom get into the kind of state that would have shocked the drawers off a duchess. It was a crying shame, I was told, and all for the want of a bit of bleach. Every time we went to visit I could tell she was itching to take to my oblivious aunt's offending S bend. When the move had been made into the newly allocated council house in Iron Mill Lane, for a while my cousins had been told they should start calling their new lavvy the bathroom because after all it was in the bathroom. Our grandmother who lived conveniently across the road with several of the younger aunts observed that nobody was going to tell her what to call the khazi and added that when she was a girl in Bethnal Green it had been called the privy. Little Violet said that at school everybody called it the toilet and to use it you had to put your hand up and ask to be excused. Apparently it had taken quite a degree of school attendance before she realised that rule only applied when you were in the classroom and so had spent a lot of time during breaks trying to find a staff member who could excuse her.

The transition from Victorian terraced housing with inconveniently placed outside conveniences to ultra-modern council housing was challenging for some people and although Old Nan seemed, rather surprisingly, to take it in her stride, most of her daughters did not. At the houses of Aunts Mag, Maud and Martha, despite the bathroom now being adjacent to the bedrooms, for several years chamber pots remained under beds. Our chamber pot was known as a Po but my aunts usually referred to theirs as a Jerry and Uncle Harold called his a Gozunder. Old Nan, rather horrifyingly to me when I was small, referred to hers as a Piss Pot. Even when I was four years old that sounded rather vulgar to me because I was never allowed to use the word Piss.

It wasn't just cleaning and toilet arrangements that made life more complicated back then. We seemed to live alongside a great many more pests than we do now. These days the sight of a marauding rodent causes a stir but then there was a tacit acceptance that vermin were just a part of life. I'm not suggesting that anyone thought they were amusing or added an entertaining dimension to life but on the other hand nobody complained too much. In summer time hundreds of flies invaded our kitchen and scullery and fly papers were hung from the ceiling and within days were liberally adorned and spotted with black mini corpses. Spiders lurked in the corners of every room, especially so in the lavatory where they grew bigger and more menacing than elsewhere and earwigs that were supposed to stick to the backyard, often crept into the house where I was told they would crawl into my ears if I wasn't careful and that was why they were called earwigs. I couldn't really tell the difference between bees and wasps but I have a feeling that the airborne striped offender that stung me so painfully in the very centre of my right hand when I was three years old and busy purloining sugar from the kitchen cupboard, was in fact a wasp. I have been wary of wasps ever since and I never made raids on the sugar again. Bees did not seem to come inside and only visited the gardens of those who grew flowers like Old Mrs Eves and Old Mrs Freeman and largely avoided those of us whose backyards were devoid of plant life.

We were plagued with mice at times and they could be heard scampering behind the walls late at night and were sometimes brazen enough to career across the kitchen floor in excited duos. My mother then laid traps baited with bits of dry bread but would never waste cheese on them. Old Nan said bugger feeding the bastards at all and placed mothballs in the kitchen corners instead because she said if there was one thing mice could not abide it was mothballs. Unlike today, back then they were not considered dangerous items. However, the best deterrent as far as mice were concerned was most definitely acquiring a cat and so at various times we did so and then became free of mice almost overnight. When our irksome household mice were replaced by decidedly more irksome household rats one year, our cat Tom the Mouse Hunter became overnight a Rat Hunter Supreme and grew ever stronger and more intimidating on a diet of larger rodents. Tom was not a cat one could easily forge a loving relationship with, being possessed of a decidedly unpleasant nature, but he was infinitely preferable to Smudge next door who seemed terrified of the very pests he had been procured to purge. Back then, unlike domestic dogs who were largely allowed to simply be family pets, a cat was definitely a working animal and a Siamese or Persian was seen only occasionally on the doorsteps of houses in London Road .

In essence, like everyone else, we were not unduly alarmed by the wildlife around us and learned to cope with the various bugs, parasites and rodents intent upon sharing our cramped quarters. There were no enticing insect sprays on supermarket shelves to tempt us to wholesale slaughter because there were of course no supermarkets. None of us quite knew what to ask for at the hardware shop apart from mouse traps and fly papers and so the elimination progress was decidedly slow.

At our house we didn't come across Flit Guns until crickets invaded the underside of the cast iron kitchen stove. Then the chirping was so intrusive that after three or four days my mother headed to Mrs Bodycombe's Hardware Store in the High Street where she had been assured she would find the miracle of Flit. And it was indeed a miracle and thus the Crickets on our Hearth met a speedy death, as did almost anything else that could creep, crawl, or fly for the next week or so until the gun was exhausted. I often wonder what the long term consequences might have been. But of course back then we didn't give a thought to consequences either to the environment or ourselves. You could say we were just not Green enough!

A Box At The Empire

Once my father came back from the war, from time to time, providing he and my mother were on speaking terms, he would propose a special treat, either just for him and me or occasionally my young brother, like going to the Museums to look at Dinosaurs and Mummies or one that involved the whole family like the Pantomime at Chatham Empire. I must emphasise that these treats were few and far between, not only because they involved unplanned expenditure but also because as time went on he and my mother had a hard time communicating. I did not quite understand the reasons for this then but later came to realise that he was an adulterer and was reputed to have more than one Fancy Woman. This behaviour caused my mother great distress and decades later she was to say that in many ways she blamed herself and that she had never been good at forgiveness. The only thing I was aware of at the time was that she seemed to spend a great deal of time crying. Nevertheless and despite all of that, the visit to the pantomime stands out in my memory like a beacon of pure joy among more mundane treats if only because there did not appear to be the slightest hint of educational intent about it. I had become wary of educational intent.

We were to see Arthur Askey of *Hello Playmates* radio fame as the Pantomime Dame in *Jack and the Beanstalk.* From memory I think he was playing the washerwoman who somehow or other was the Giant's mother and I now have no idea who the Principal Boy was except that in true panto fashion Jack himself was to be played by a young woman. Having read a great deal about panto via Noel Streatfield I was bursting with excitement because this was to be the Treat of the decade most especially because it also featured a dance troupe of children from Crown Academy, a local theatre school. My longing to be one of those fortunate children was passionately intense.

I would like to say that the visits to various museums and art galleries had also been a resounding success but as far as I was concerned that wasn't so although my young brother had displayed a fleeting fascination with dinosaurs. Half an afternoon in the Egyptian Room at the British Museum had been bearable but not riveting and neither of us found paintings all that thrilling. Our Grandmother was heard to say that in her opinion it was the war that had ruined my father. Aunt Rose who was married to a gallery-visiting Welshman said this was because sometimes wars turned perfectly ordinary men from normal to highbrow. In her opinion they returned to Civvy Street with ideas above their station and this was evidenced by the development of an admiration for foreign ideas. I was wont to agree with her there because my father seemed to have a preoccupation with something called spaghetti, most definitely a very foreign food, which he insisted was delicious, and I privately thought looked like worms in blood. To be fair the only spaghetti I had actually seen was the tinned variety courtesy of Heinz, a poster of which was displayed on the outside wall of Penny, Son & Parkers' shop adjacent to the Roman Catholic Church on The Hill. When I pointed out the similarity with worms my father told me that I was extremely foolish if I thought that Heinz canned spaghetti was anything like the real thing. The real thing, he said, tasted of sunshine and olives and tomatoes that burst with sweetness. Not knowing what olives might be I made no further response but decided that I would be most unlikely to ever sample the real thing and in fact would actively avoid it at all costs.

It was to be a long time before I was given the opportunity to do so when a boyfriend took me to an Italian restaurant in Bloomsbury on the occasion of his own birthday. I was sharply reminded of the worms just before cautiously sampling a first surprisingly tasty mouthful. I then came to the realization that all things Italian were not necessarily as unpalatable as they had previously appeared to be. Sometime later in discussion with a cousin whose father had also been ruined by the war, far from enthusiastically agreeing, she said that she didn't think she could ever get used to foreign muck and would prefer a Wimpy with chips any day of the week.

But when I was still a child these discussions were not frequent because we rarely went in for what is now termed Eating Out and on those exceptional occasions when we did, it was generally in cafes serving Egg & Chips which I learned we might be having, all being well, after the much vaunted visit to the theatre. This dining experience was to be in a café known to my father, just around the corner from the theatre. The town of Chatham was definitely his patch. He had been born there, abandoned by his mother there as an infant and brought up there in a Roman Catholic orphanage and as a result knew every inch of the central streets and alleyways. He had fond memories of being taken in groups each December to pantomimes at The Empire courtesy of local philanthropists. There were times apparently when these annual treats stretched to fish and chip suppers for those boys who proved themselves to be extra especially well behaved and my father strove hard to ensure he was always included. He was therefore left with an enduring fondness for the theatre.

The Empire had been designed by a famous theatre architect called Frank Matcham, he told me, for Oswald Stoll and had first opened in 1912 on the site of a previous theatre called The Gaiety. As Chatham was a naval town, Matcham had given The Empire a nautical theme and it boasted an eighty foot long façade and an imposing dome resting on pillars on which was mounted a sailing ship. When it first opened the variety shows featured one star after another and as a boy my father had been privileged to see not only Marie Lloyd and Harry Lauder but also the great Houdini himself. In more recent years stars such as Gracie Fields, George Formby and Phyllis Dixie all trod The Empire's stage.

Even Old Nan was grudgingly impressed that we were to become proper theatre-goers and said she had seen Todd Slaughter's famous melodrama there with her Edgar, *Sweeny Todd, the Demon Barber of Fleet Street* not just once but twice because they had been so taken with it. What's more she had heard that Max Miller was to appear there after Christmas and everybody knew he brought in packed houses. My mother, engrossed in knitting a work sock for my father, sniffed a bit and said that was because he was known for being smutty and she couldn't abide him not even on the wireless. My Grandmother acknowledged that smutty he might be but he was also comical and the Lord knew we could all do with a bleeding laugh from time to time. The steel knitting needles snapped and clicked disapprovingly.

We set off for Chatham a few days later, just a week before Christmas, in our best clothes. My mother wore her black court shoes with heels that made her appear just a little taller and more intimidating and Velouty for Beauty was carefully applied to her cheeks then a judicious line of Crimson Sunset to her lips. My father strutted importantly in his demob suit and striped tie with a white silk scarf around his neck and he excitedly winked at me once or twice. We set off by train from Gravesend and arrived at The Empire Box Office with half an hour to spare before the matinee performance was to begin. Family groups swarmed about the lobby, mothers clutching tickets and impatient children hopping from foot to foot and asking if it was nearly time to go in. I felt completely tight inside with excitement and anticipation because I was suddenly a child that Noel Streatfield herself might have recognised, a child being taken to the theatre, the Real Theatre and not simply The Majestic Cinema in Gravesend. Surely the leap towards dancing lessons and a possible career on the stage could now not be so very far away! I did a small experimental pirouette and thought possibly I might even turn out to be one of those astonishing children like Petrova Fossil in *Ballet Shoes* and possessed of natural ability.

It was then that my father found that all tickets for the stalls and circle had been sold, pre-sold in fact. Listening carefully I wondered what that could possibly mean and further learned that in fact the only seats left in the house were five in a Box at the huge sum of four pounds. A squabble immediately broke out between my parents with my mother maintaining that had he thought ahead my father would have booked like anybody with any sense and that it stood to reason that nobody could afford four pounds. His shoulders sagged a little making the silk scarf swing forlornly from side to side and those still waiting to pick up tickets safely booked ahead tut tutted with the slight irritation that people always have in queues that are momentarily not proceeding forward as they should. So we moved aside and the argument continued under the faded wine and gold awnings at the side of the foyer.

I watched nervously as the confident ticket-clasping groups handed them over, some to the man in the navy and gold uniform who stood guarding the door that said Stalls and some to the woman who wore a jaunty cap and directed the way up the curved stairway to the Circle. The crowd began to thin considerably and the woman in the ticket office was beginning to sort ten shilling notes from pounds and make piles of half-crown pieces. My mother stopped speaking in an unnaturally loud voice and said that she had noticed that *Snow White* was showing at the pictures just along the road and little Bernard hadn't ever seen it and was sure to enjoy it. My chest began to feel uncomfortably tight then because I certainly didn't want to see *Snow White* under any circumstances. I wanted to be a theatre going child and see *Jack and the Beanstalk* starring Arthur Askey. And more than anything I desperately wanted to see those oh so fortunate child dancers being trained for a glittering future. I began to cry quietly and leaned against my mother's Sunday best navy wool coat inherited from

Aunt Mag who had put on so much weight after the birth of little Ann Elizabeth. My mother grabbed my shoulder and pushed me towards my father advising him to witness how much he had upset me. This was unlike her and therefore quite alarming. He looked at me unblinkingly, swaying a little from side to side and his shoulders drooped a little more. I took the opportunity to produce two or three shuddering sobs and was aware of a slow viscous trickle down my right cheek. I knew he was aware of it too.

There was further discussion, this time in low voices and I heard him say that it was a good thing he had been paid the day before and that it had included a bonus for Christmas. And so to my mother's amazement and it was certainly something she talked about a great deal over the following months most especially with my grandmother and aunts, he went back to the box office and handed over a crisp pink five pound note. I followed close at his heels in disbelief at what was happening because at once it seemed that we were going to be theatre goers after all. In fact we were the very last patrons to be ushered up the curving staircase that afternoon and led importantly through a low arched doorway into our very own Box overlooking the Chatham Empire stage. There were five seats in a row, covered in red velour, deep and luxurious and the walls of the little room were draped in heavy red and gold curtains. We found ourselves seated only minutes before the lights dimmed and the performance began.

It was my very first experience of a Real Theatre, my introduction to the tradition of Pantomime other than what I had read in books and I was immediately very much taken with the Principal Boy and the Pantomime Dame and the ritualistic heckling from the audience. It was hard to believe that I was seeing the famous Arthur Askey who had previously been just a voice on the radio whose jokes were difficult to understand. But of course most exciting of all were the child actors and dancers in their astonishing costumes confidently performing alongside the adults, sometimes holding hands with Arthur Askey himself. I longed to be one of them with a longing so powerful that it was physically painful.

During the intermission a woman dressed in black with a little white apron and cap brought us a pot of coffee which my father said didn't taste as if it was Camp Essence together with some biscuits and orange juice which we didn't have to pay for. It was included in the price of our Box Seats which my mother thought was the very least they could do considering how much the seats had cost. The cups were very small, a further criticism because it would have been Daylight Robbery had it not been for Free. I remember very little of the meal we had later in the café that had been there since my father was a boy except that my brother fell asleep and was unable to eat his chips. On the way home my father and I stood together in the train corridor, not because the train was crowded but simply because we felt like it. He asked me if I had enjoyed my first theatre trip and I nodded vigorously. I nodded because I had enjoyed it so very much that I could not trust myself to speak without bursting into tears. Finally I managed to tell him that it had been the very best day of my whole life and he looked pleased, pushed his shoulders back and put on his chirpy look. He asked me which bit I had liked best and I said the best bits of all were the tap dancing children from Crown Academy closely followed by the woman dressed like a maid who brought us the tray of coffee and orange juice during the intermission. He asked what I had thought of Arthur Askey and I said that I'd liked him very much, mostly because he was famous but I hadn't liked him quite as much as the Crown Academy dance troupe.

It had been a completely astonishingly exciting day that I longed to repeat so I asked when we might be able to go to the theatre again. I was told that at some stage, perhaps next year, we might go to a performance of *Peter Pan* and we would do it all Properly by booking seats in advance. This all sounded very promising. Nevertheless it was to be a long time before I would find myself back at The Chatham Empire when in 1958 I would go with a songwriter called Bill Crompton to see a performance of his great friend and ally, Morgan Thunderclap Jones, a pianist who had thoughtfully provided us with complimentary seats in the front stalls. On that occasion there was the added excitement of actually visiting Morgan's dressing room which was predictably cramped and tiny because he wasn't exactly a Star Performer. It was the very first theatre dressing room I was to find myself inside, however and therefore thrilling and exhilarating in its own right. The theatre was exactly as I remembered it but it wasn't to remain so. At the end of the 1950s a change of management decided to convert it into a cabaret venue and removed the original fixed seating in the orchestra stalls, replacing it all with ornate little round tables and chairs. This idea was received with little enthusiasm and some evenings there were more staff in the place than customers. The decision to close The Empire was taken early in 1960 and shortly before the due date the electricity was cut off due to unpaid bills despite a much advertised closing performance which apparently had sold out in advance. The theatre never reopened and a couple of years later it was sold for redevelopment along with other adjacent buildings. It was finally demolished and today the site is a car park serving local government offices.

My mother always remained firmly keener on visits to the cinema than to theatres and said a fair amount of money could be wasted on highfaluting box seats which was of course a point hard to argue with. One of her reasons for her preference was the fact that in a proper theatre it was almost impossible to unwrap a boiled sweet or a chocolate without others turning their disapproving gaze upon you. That kind of censure simply didn't happen at The Majestic in Gravesend which made going to the Pictures an altogether more relaxing affair. There was no doubt at all that she had enjoyed our theatre visit a great deal less than I had. I was never to forget the magic of that afternoon when we saw the famous Arthur Askey in *Jack & The Beanstalk* together with the supporting troupe of child performers from the luxury of a Box overlooking the stage at the Chatham Empire, exactly like a family in a book!

The School Blazer

I was in my last year at St Botolph's when the newish and decidedly tyrannical headmaster decided that what the school needed to lift it above those lesser academic establishments in the district was a uniform and an anthem. Mr Cook was a man with an ambitious agenda for making sweeping improvements to the school. This did not simply include compelling we students, and with an undoubted all-embracing flow-on effect in mind for the adults in our lives, to focus upon what he called the Rich Tapestry of our Kentish heritage; oh no, it extended into areas we might not have dreamed of previously. A number of hitherto long overlooked local traditions were to be resurrected. Although I have now forgotten what most of them were, at the time of course I listened carefully along with everyone else because we were very much afraid of the man.

Our joint academic performance was to be immediately lifted, by force if necessary, and the headmaster himself would personally teach Mathematics to those of us approaching the greatly dreaded Eleven Plus exam. His style of teaching as previously documented included a great deal of shouting, kicking desk tops onto fingers and becoming alarmingly puce in the face. This educational technique ensured that even the previously most disruptive and disorderly boys became lamb-like overnight. It was to be more than fifty years before I came to realise that this dread and dislike of him extended also into the staff. Our much loved class teacher, Mr Will Clarke, in email correspondence eons on revealed just how profoundly the new headmaster had affected his life, with general bullying and demands involving a great deal of his personal time. He was indeed a man who successfully instilled fear and loathing into the hearts and minds of all who were unfortunate enough to cross his path.

We were told about the proposed School Anthem on a Thursday morning at an unusual assembly. It was explained to us that our Old School would in years to come be known to us as our alma mater and the anthem we were about to learn was a patronal song. This of course meant nothing whatsoever to us. Mr Cook added that the famous Charterhouse School sang *Jerusalem*, Dover Grammar School sang *Thou Whose Almighty Word*, The Liverpool Blue Coat School sang *Praise to the Lord, the Almighty* and Magdalen College School sang *The Lilies of the Field*. We children of St Botolph's, Northfleet Hill who knew nothing of the worthy establishments that tripped from his tongue were to sing *Front to the Northern Breeze* recently composed by himself with some assistance from Mrs Frost the pianist. There followed a twenty minute rehearsal of a mournful hymn-like refrain which began with `...*At St Botolph's School on the hill we stand with our front to the northern breeze....*' and about which I recall nothing further. We were told that we should run through what we had just sung, in our heads over the next few days and be mindful that by Monday next our singing had to be flawless.

The following day at yet another unusual assembly, this time held at the end of the day rather than the beginning, we were told about the School Blazer which Helen Gunner the vicar's daughter modelled for us looking both important and embarrassed as she did so.

This garment, the colour described as maroon and later called wine-red by my mother, was undoubtedly smart, double breasted with gold buttons. It could be ordered directly from the school for a mere twenty-two shillings and sixpence apiece. We ten and eleven year-olds in particular, were to emphasise to our parents that a St Botolph's School Blazer was an absolute necessity. A notice was handed to each of us which we must ensure was passed on with immediacy as soon as we got home. An order form was attached which should be filled in by an adult as speedily as possible. Significant penalties might be incurred by those children who simply abandoned this important notice in a pocket.

Later that evening, relaxed after a Friday tea of fish and chips, my father commented that a School Blazer was not an altogether bad idea and it would certainly define the wearer as a pupil of a school that Cared. That fellow Cook was no sluggard and was trying to do Right by his pupils no matter how much girls like me objected to his bad temper. Possibly he was going to be exactly what we needed to ensure that we gave the Eleven Plus examination our very best shot. My mother was doubtful and pointed out that it was over a guinea and I wasn't going to be able to wear it at my next school whether I passed the Eleven Plus or whether I didn't because the Grammar School colours were navy and white and the Secondary Modern were green and white. She discussed it a day or two later with Grace Bennett in order to ascertain if a blazer was to be purchased for her Joan but apparently no decision had yet been made. Molly Freeman said that there was no chance whatsoever that she or her brother George would become the proud owners of blazers. Jennifer Berryman's grandmother had definitely agreed to the new item of clothing, however, and was going to take her to the photographer in the High Street to have her photographed wearing it. Pearl Banfield's parents were also in favour which pacified Pearl who had been getting more and more anxious over the weekend as to what might happen to those of us whose parents did not respond in the affirmative. A few days later to my surprise I was to find it had been decided that I would also become a proud blazer-owner which I have to admit was something of a relief. Within three weeks it transpired that more than two thirds of St Botolph's Eleven Plus Year 1951 were to be blazer-clad and mostly completely paid for before very long. Photographs were taken for the Gravesend & Dartford Reporter of us singing *Front to the Northern Breeze* and Mr Cook was quoted as confidently expecting a very satisfactory exam result.

The idea of blazer owning had certainly added a dimension of excitement to the school day for a large part of the term and protected the wearers from the outer extremes of the headmaster's temper frenzies. Most of his fury was now more specifically directed towards those who remained blazerless, particularly the boys who were kicked and slapped with cheerful regularity. After a while the maroon jackets, once so carefully hanger-hung in parental wardrobes, were more carelessly slung on hooks in hallways or at the bottom of stairs. My mother even stopped telling me to take mine off the moment I got home from school. This was just as well because by the end of the term its right hand pocket had become the home of my pet mouse, Timothy Gunner.

Some progressive parents back then allowed their children to own pet mice and even bought little packets of mixed seed to supplement table scraps and provided birthday presents of mouse homes in the form of new-fangled metal cages from the pet shop in Gravesend. Predictably perhaps, mine were not among them. Generally speaking my mother was not overly fond of animals and even found it difficult to extend much affection to the family dog. She could just about tolerate cats and had no time at all for the tortoise my father once gave me, breathing an audible sigh of relief when it perished during its first ever period of hibernation. A pet mouse was out of the question and I knew better than to even pose the question.

So I would never have become a mouse owner in the first place if Helen Gunner the vicar's daughter, whose parents were of the progressive variety, had not had to give up her beloved pet when her family made their final arrangements to move on to a new parish in far-off Bermuda. I inherited Timothy Gunner with great delight and solemnly promised Helen that his name would never be changed because he was now used to it. Sadly his cage, home-made by the vicar himself, was going with them. Housing Timothy Gunner became a dilemma and that was how he came to live in the right hand pocket of the maroon school blazer. This arrangement worked extremely well for several weeks and Timothy Gunner behaved beautifully during school hours, sleeping peacefully and not drawing undue attention to himself except at playtime when other girls lined up to admire him and offer him bits of broken biscuit. When I got home he would happily explore the bedroom floor and as long as I left the blazer close by could be relied upon to return to it. Later in the evening he and the jacket would be hung on a bottom-of-the-stairs hook. I have no idea what he did during the night but he was always safely nestled in the pocket in the morning.

The ownership of my first ever pet mouse had been surprisingly stress-free and I even began to wonder why anyone thought mice needed cages. Was it not even quite cruel to confine a white mouse to a cage? At some stage I might write a letter of enquiry to the RSPCA. So all was well until the fateful Saturday morning when I skipped happily down to Molly's house to exchange gossip about film stars, and returned to find the maroon blazer missing from its hook. Casually enquiring as to its whereabouts I was struck mute when told by my father that it had been taken to the dry cleaner in Northfleet High Street. My mother, it appeared, had decided it was becoming very dirty and smelly – smelly enough to be in need of dry cleaning. But we were not a family that ever used the services of the dry cleaner and the news made my throat suddenly very dry indeed. When I regained my voice I pointed out that I hadn't noticed the smell – what kind of smell was it? It was like ammonia I was told, and later my mother herself said she would have very much liked to know what on earth I had been doing with it to get it into such a state. And to think it had cost over a guinea too not to mention that the dry cleaning would be half a crown. When it returned I was never, ever to let it get into that kind of condition again.

In panic I headed for the library and asked the mystified librarian where the section on dry cleaning was but of course there wasn't one. Where then might I find information on what was entailed during a common or garden dry cleaning process? She looked annoyed and said it wasn't a topic that involved many enquiries. An elderly borrower lingering in the General Science Section said he believed various chemicals were used but was unclear as to what they might be. Ammonia might be one of them though. No he did not know if the process might be dangerous to mice. I was crying huge and bitter tears as I retraced my steps down Dover Road so much so that old Mrs Eves waiting at the bus stop asked me what on earth the problem was and looked puzzled when I said my mother had taken my school blazer to the dry cleaner's. That was nothing to get so het up about she sagely advised.

 I waited anxiously for the return of the blazer some days later, now in a paper package and hung on a metal hanger, smelling of lemons and lavender and nicely pressed. In horrified anticipation of a mangled mouse corpse I inspected the right hand pocket as nonchalantly as possible. It was empty. It was as if Timothy Gunner had never existed in the first place. Henceforth on each school morning I donned the maroon blazer I began to cry and could provide no convincing explanation as to why this was.

Homes For The Worthy Poor

My mother was born in 1908 and could clearly remember the flurry of building projects that followed the Great War and known as the Homes for Heroes. Ten years later at local Council meetings these developments were referred to as Homes for the Worthy Poor, but never in the presence of those they were intended to house of course. Whether for heroes or the humble I don't think it ever occurred to the young Constants of Crayford that they might ever be fortunate enough to live in one and in any case they were happy enough to have a proper roof over their heads in Maxim Road. I say proper roof because the older girls, Maggie and Nellie could certainly remember a time when home was a tarpaulin in the corner of a ploughed field and Crayford itself was situated in rural Kent and not in Greater London as, rather astonishingly, it seems to be today. The Homes for Heroes, where even the less desirable residences were equipped with hot water geysers and baths very nearly hidden in kitchen alcoves, were a step up from the basic facilities the older girls were accustomed to. Such details were probably not noticed by the younger children.

For instance when I was very small it did not occur to me that there was anything remotely undesirable about our house at 28 York Road, nestled as it was in the lower third of the South side of the street. It was simply home and to me when I was two, three and four years of age, invariably welcoming. Similar homes had been built since the eighteenth century, tight rows of neatly constructed two-up-two-down cottages beginning their stretch almost from the central point of tidy English towns, extending to their outskirts and very nearly encroaching into what was by the middle of the twentieth century, to be called the Suburbs. Unlike other European countries, England's towns largely lacked centrally built tall blocks of flats that unwillingly gave way to terraces and ultimately more widely spaced homes. The latter, whether Council or privately constructed, had to await their advent for some considerable time. Strangely, this did not appear to be the case in Scotland however, where lofty blocks rose menacingly and earlier from the very centre of both Edinburgh and Glasgow and very possibly other places also. Stubbornly, however, English cities, even those as swarmingly jam-packed as Liverpool and Manchester, opted for back-to-back structures and crowded courts rather than buildings that were too alarmingly vertical. So the English remained blissfully unaware of congested centrally-placed apartments such as those gracing the back streets of Berlin, Paris and Prague until they had enough disposable cash with which to travel. which was, of course, going to be quite a long time into the future.

By the time I was six years old though, I was beginning to compare our house in Northfleet unfavourably with that of my Aunt Mag in Iron Mill Lane, Crayford. Close to the Three Jolly Farmers pub and the 480 bus stop to and from Gravesend, it was part of an estate hastily built in the early years of the twentieth century to house local factory workers. This was at a time when Industrial Crayford erupted from its previous state as a rather sleepy village. The change came with extraordinary rapidity, so much so that decades later unmistakable signs of a previously more rustic life still pervaded the very air of the place. These were facts that did not concern me in the slightest at the time. My immense admiration for the house in Iron Mill Lane was simply because it was semi-detached, rather than part of a terrace, it had its own little entrance hall, rather than forcing entry directly into the Front Room, and wonder of wonders, it had a bathroom complete with indoor lavatory! It also had an almond tree in the little front garden which in the spring burst into creamy blossom and made passers-by pause and comment upon its magnificence.

The house was not only conveniently placed for the frequent visits to the Jolly Farmers that my grandmother and aunts seemed so attached to, it was also handy for my Uncle Harold's job at Vickers where the work itself was of such importance to the War that he was exempted from service and where he was progressing rapidly towards becoming a Foreman. As Aunt Mag was fond of pointing out, Vickers would be hard pressed to do without him. My oldest cousin, Young Harold explained to me that this was something to do with Vickers making munitions which you needed if you were going to fight a war. My own father had been Called Up because his job was only at Bevan's Cement Works and the war could do without cement very well. I didn't really understand what munitions were or all that much about cement but I listened politely.

My mother was of the firm opinion that Big Harold her brother-in-law was one of the weak and cowardly and in the previous combat would undoubtedly have been sent a white feather. She went further and maintained that he had even run to his foreman and begged to be transferred to Essential Work. As she made these dubious comments frequently about men who had not been sent to the Front no-one paid much attention to her. It could be safely said that Nellie Hendy had a relentlessly unforgiving attitude towards those males who to all intents and purposes were healthy yet had not been required to enlist. Why couldn't Essential work be carried out by women she would have liked to know or if that was impossible then by the maimed who had emerged from the previous war?

However, the cowardly were destined to be forgotten even by her when my brother was born and I reached my seventh birthday because the war itself was fast fading into memory. Even my father, who had loved his years of service, had reluctantly returned to take his place once more within the ranks of Bevans' workers. I now listened with interest to Sunday afternoon conversations between my parents concerning Housing Lists and how to move up them, and perhaps moving to Erith or Crayford or Dartford where smart new houses were being built. To aid this proposed move the Council officials in each area had listed us together with the fact that we were living in grossly overcrowded circumstances with, variously, Aunts Mag or Maud or Martha. Council Officers visited the homes of each of these aunts and inspected the sofas upon which my parents were supposedly sleeping and the topping and tailing my cousins and I were purportedly doing. It was always decided that our need was indeed worthy. A new home was not going to appear overnight, however.

My father was keen to stay reasonably close to Northfleet in order to cycle to his shifts at Bevans and also for ease of the nostalgia trips he was fond of making to Chatham where he had grown up. My mother, however, seemed quite drawn to the innovative Tin Houses, with corrugated iron roofs that were planned for Erith because she did not want to have to live in the pockets of That Crayford Lot if she could avoid it. It would be true to say that she had an oddly symbiotic relationship with her sisters. I simply wanted a house with a bathroom and if I had actually been in a position to make a choice, I would have chosen a prefab identical to those in Orchard Road close by the Northfleet cemetery and the Old Rec where the first tenants had been happily living since March 1946. Sadly my mother did not fancy a prefab at all because not only did they look cold and uninviting, more importantly they had been built with the help of German prisoners of war and you never knew what that might entail in the long run because you couldn't be too careful.

Two girls from my class at school, Jean Taylor and Wendy Selves, lived in the smart new prefabs that were bursting with modern conveniences, known as mod cons. They were such good friends that they went everywhere together and even finished each other's sentences which was fascinating. They did not look alike because Jean was tall and fair whilst Wendy was small and dark but they tried to be as similar as possible by copying each other. Each had hair I greatly envied, twisted in rags at night so as to form long ringlets in the morning. I had actually seen inside Wendy's prefab on the heady occasion when she invited me to a special afternoon tea at which her mother had served fish paste sandwiches and Lyons fruit pies cut into quarters. I had looked inside the bathroom and taken note of the pale green tiles and reassured myself that they really did have an indoor toilet. I told Wendy that I greatly admired their prefab and ventured to enquire if the fact that it had been partly built by prisoners of war concerned her mother at all. Wendy said she didn't know what I was talking about and no prisoners of any kind had been anywhere near their prefab at any time whatsoever and I was mad if I thought so. This seemed just a tiny bit odd as this was a year in which POWs featured rather more than previously in the life of the local population. As a community we were being gently encouraged to see the Germans as human beings rather than as hideous monsters. A service for them had been recently held at Chalk Church during which hymns were sung in both German and English. The sermon was preached in German and the local Vicar obligingly translated it into English. In return, to show goodwill POWs did their best to fight a fire in a local fifteenth century cottage and managed to save a great many antiques and ensure that the damage was restricted to the upper storey only. All this did nothing to improve my mother's attitude toward them and when an unexploded bomb was found in Albion Terrace, Gravesend and had to be defused she promptly laid the blame solely upon the attendees at the Chalk Church service, even suggesting they had absconded from their camp in the small hours and deliberately placed it. This sounded unlikely even to me but I didn't say so.

Eventually, to my mother's delight, we were offered a house with a corrugated roof, close to the bus route, at Erith and in great excitement we went by motor bike and side-car to visit the site one afternoon at the end of my father's Six-to-Two shift. Erith lies on the banks of the Thames, like Gravesend and Northfleet except closer to London and the history of the town is similarly tied to the river. There was once a royal dockyard there and there was still an impressively long pier in early 1948 where we sat that afternoon eating sandwiches and drinking cold tea from lemonade bottles. My father, who at the time seemed particularly driven to giving mini-lectures of an improving and educational nature, told me that the name Erith was Saxon in origin and that Henry VIII founded a naval dockyard there and that furthermore one of his most famous warships was built there and he only wished he could recall the name of it but for the life of him he couldn't. What he could remember though was that the famous local Callenders Cable Factory provided a great deal of employment in the town and of course everybody knew that it was Callenders who had laid an underwater pipeline in the Channel and it was this very pipeline that had supplied the fuel used by Allied vehicles during the D Day Landings in June 1944. I nodded in what I hoped was an enthusiastic manner but thought this was an excruciatingly boring bit of information.

My mother bringing a lighter note to the exchange observed that Great Aunt Martha, now living in Northfleet, remembered Erith well when it was something of a Resort and had gone there on day trips as a very small child either on a pleasure steamer or a train. Her father had on one such occasion won her a wax doll with long curly hair at a kiosk, which, tragically, she had lost on the way home but had never forgotten. This was much more interesting and my heart bled for the child that Great Aunt Martha, known to me as Little Nanny, had once been. Just imagine the horror of losing a wax doll with long curly hair!

Like comparable riverside towns, despite its romantic heritage, Erith was ultimately destined to become an industrial centre mainly due to the conveniently placed docks and its proximity to both central London and the English Channel. It was during the late Victorian period that two entrepreneurs in particular, Charles Beadle and William Anderson, ensured that the place abandoned all aspirations to remain a Resort and became instead the foremost industrial area of the South East, engineering emerging as its most prominent industry.

The houses we had come to see turned out to be something of a disappointment to my parents. On the outskirts of the town, the rows of imposingly large homes, each with a red-brown undulating roof, looked acceptable enough to me although startlingly different from York Road. I asked if every house had a bathroom and a hallway and when I was ignored I asked again. I had to ask three times before my mother looked distractedly in my direction briefly and simply nodded saying that they were bound to have and no mistake. My father said they were further from Bevans than he had hoped but he had heard there were good jobs going at Vickers. My mother said when it rained the din on those roofs would be awful and she wondered if her nerves would be able to stand it. She would ask the Doctor for his advice next time she went and then hesitantly added that she couldn't help noticing that the rows of little houses closer to the town centre looked a much better bet. I was surprised by this revelation because the terraces that looked so very similar to York Road did not seem big enough to accommodate a bathroom and a hallway which was worrying. I also wondered why the Doctor had to be asked for advice and decided that maybe he had to write us a letter before we would be able to procure the tenancy of one of these new houses with the wavy roofs.

A week or so later I heard her in discussion with one of my aunts and it appeared that the Doctor had strongly advised that we should go nowhere near the Tin Houses at Erith. The reasons were various. For one thing the din on the roofs when it rained was indeed bound to be something awful and for another they were built far too close to the river and it stood to reason that the damp rising off the water on a winter morning played Merry Hell with the chest. What was more, Little Jean was known as delicate to the Doctor and the wind around the Tin Houses in winter was certain to cause pneumonia. Quite apart from all that they were a long way from Bevans and everybody knew that Bevans paid better than either Vickers or Callenders. Besides, there were bound to be lovely new estates going up any time now much closer to Northfleet. You only had to look at Kings Farm to see that because that entire estate went up in no time at all.

So we did not end up living at Erith in a Tin House and although I mourned the loss of the entrance hall and the bathroom I was glad not to have to change schools and leave the groups of children I knew, even those who were greatly hated and definitely my enemies. During the years that followed there was frequent animated discussion concerning housing and parental conversation was littered with talk of moving to Painters Ash, Istead Rise or Valley Drive but we never did. Long after I had permanently left the area my mother even cautiously considered applying for a tenancy in one of the new high rise flats that were a mere stone's throw from her garden gate and were climbing rapidly skyward. She thought she might like to live on the very top floor and awake to an astonishing vista each morning but within a very short space of time, predictably perhaps, she changed her mind.

The much-vaunted move from number twenty-eight did not in fact become a reality until the latter part of the 1960s when residents were advised that the south side of our street was to be demolished to make way for a complex of modern units to house young families. Within a very short space of time my mother moved with her cat, Simon, to Wallis Park, situated on the site of Huggens College in Northfleet. She realised almost immediately that she was going to hate living there and nothing could convince her otherwise despite the smart entrance hall and brand new bathroom. She even complained about the dreadful din on the roof whenever it rained. A further move to Painters Ash, where the entrance hall and bathroom were decidedly smaller and more cramped, proved much more successful. She was even sure that the rainfall was infinitely less invasive there. And when I visited one afternoon I could not help but notice that in the patch of garden immediately adjacent to her front door was an almond tree that when in blossom apparently caused passers-by to pause and make admiring comment.

Words & Music

My cousins June and Pat went to the same school in Crayford and had the same likes and dislikes, at times even insisting on wearing the same shoe style and pretending to be sisters rather than cousins. For a number of years their favourite poem was, *If all the world was paper and all the sea was ink, and all the trees were bread and cheese, what would we have to drink?* which they chanted frequently with linked arms whilst executing a little hopping dance. Of course I quickly learned it from them though I can't say it ever became a favourite with me because I was a firm admirer of Robert Louis Stevenson at the time. Somewhat surprisingly my mother also seemed to share my admiration for him but said that her all-time favourite poem was *Meg Merrilies* which she had learned as an eight-year-old at the very same Roman Catholic school her nieces now went to during one of the winter periods when she and her sisters had been allowed to attend on a more or less regular basis. This was of course back in the days when teaching nuns had a serious reputation for sadism and the Constant children, prone to sudden desertion of the entire idea of compulsory education during times when peas, beans, fruit and hops might be harvested, were not popular. I was told that by the late 1940s the Sisters of Mercy had greatly improved their overall attitude and children were chastised and tormented less frequently and with less enthusiasm.

My cousin Margaret who was six years older than me and therefore very worldly was not terribly keen on poetry but she had a favourite song that she sang a great deal. It concerned someone called Bobby Shafto who had gone to sea wearing silver buckles and eventually was going to return to marry her. I privately thought it a rather silly song but sang along with her in order to please her. Her second favourite song was *Bye Bye Blackbird* and more to my liking.

We were in those years exposed to a range of words and music that today have largely disappeared. Music encircled us but it was a collective experience rather than that which today's child might be accustomed to, where a background of popular song is savoured for minutes at a time on mobile phones and iPads. Songs and jingles were learned first from our mothers and then from school and then from each other but the melodies that most preoccupied us came from The Wireless and even the poorest home possessed one and so our music was also the music of our friends and neighbours. Everyone listened to the wireless whether actively or in a more preoccupied manner for most of the day.

Music While You Work, a half hour programme featuring non-stop popular tunes twice daily, mid-morning and mid-afternoon, reigned supreme and every household in Northfleet tuned in. Those with more upmarket tastes and a yen to become socially upwardly mobile, whose ranks I aimed to join, were able to sample the delights of *Desert Island Discs* presented by the legendary Roy Plomley and thus occasionally we listened to Chopin waltzes and Richard Tauber singing light opera. When I inadvisably told one of my older cousins that Chopin was so beautiful it made me cry she looked at me curiously and said I must be daft but Margaret explained to her it was just because I was highbrow which was what my father had become and nothing to be proud of.

For the highbrow or lowbrow and all in-between, The Wireless inevitably became The Radio at some stage in the 1950s when it was only referred to as The Wireless by people of our parents' age who were decidedly old-fashioned and vaguely embarrassing. Our particular model was very similar to those in the houses on either side of us, a large polished wooden box that might almost have been classed as a piece of furniture in its own right if only a little bigger. It evidenced its importance with its stylish design, contoured and rounded and highly polished with an important looking speaker dominating its face. A number of knobs and a dial sat smugly below the speaker. One knob simply turned the set on and off and twisting to the right adjusted the volume. Another, used much less frequently, searched for stations, listed temptingly and mysteriously and sounding like destinations on some long distance European train trip. A smaller knob of a different shape altered the tone and another selected long, medium or short wave. I think it was a Murphy Model 674 and it had cost an astonishing nine guineas when purchased in a sale in 1939, a joint wedding gift to my parents from a group of the Crayford aunts. Later I learned that my youngest aunt, the much derided Freda, had managed to get her name included on the card but had failed to contribute to the purchase which apparently was Just Like Her! Despite this sad confusion concerning a most significant wedding gift, the Wireless immediately became a prized possession and was given its own specially built shelf in the corner of our kitchen, high enough to ensure that I wasn't able to fiddle with its knobs, which I longed to do. And to ensure the continuity of on-call news and music all that was henceforth needed was the broadcasting license which cost a not inconsiderable ten shillings a year until it doubled in 1946 becoming one pound! According to Old Nan who had suggested the set as a suitable wedding present in the first place, this development was nothing short of Daylight Bleeding Robbery. Rightly or wrongly we wireless owners could not take our daily dose of news and music completely for granted in those days.

During the war years more modestly designed radio receivers were available for scores of hurriedly wed young couples and they had knobs only for volume, tuning and on/off. Presumably these were made to government specifications and were unable to receive long wave which ensured that we British would be protected from German propaganda. As I grew older I became increasingly fascinated by the wide range of European radio stations that could apparently be appraised and more than a little peeved that my mother seemed disinclined to avail herself of the opportunity to try them. This had not been the case during the war when we regularly listened to Radio Hamburg becoming more and more infuriated by what the dastardly Germans were telling us. Not, I hasten to explain, that I understood any of these developments but I was more than aware of what I should think and believe. Not a day went by without a relative or neighbour reinforcing the fact that Adolf Hitler needed to be Strung Up and that generally speaking all things German would contaminate normal decent people like us if we got too close to them. That was why breathing the same air as POWs was particularly dangerous and so we must cross the road if we saw a group of them heading towards us bent upon some community work project. These were facts and the BBC confirmed our prejudices on a daily basis, there being in those days no local radio where alternative views from the man in the street might be expressed. Sometime after the war when a new channel was launched called The Third Programme I would have liked to investigate it properly but my mother claimed that it gave her the creeps.

When she and her sisters were children, before the advent of regular broadcasting, music for the working classes was that which they created for themselves via sing-songs in the pub on Friday and Saturday nights starting with *Two Lovely Black Eyes* and ending with *Roll Out The Barrel*. Everyone knew the words and prescribed order and even as the decades passed the ritual changed little so that the youngest of us listening from our beds in the late 1940s were comforted by the familiar sounds drifting from nearby locals like The Volley.

Those Northfleet families aspiring towards the lower middle classes and perhaps living in Springhead Road rather than Shepherd Street had at some stage wisely invested in pianos for their parlours and held more genteel sing-songs without the aid of beer or gin. Their repertoires were also more refined featuring such numbers as *Come Into The Garden Maud* and *I'll Walk Beside You*. My grandmother who was completely familiar with most popular music hall numbers viewed these parlour songs with more than a little suspicion regularly noting that they were more suited to the Toffs than the likes of us. It was undoubtedly due to her background of singing for the amusement of theatre queues that I became word perfect in such numbers as *Waiting At The Church, Boiled Beef and Carrots* and *Oh, Oh Antonio* by the time I was three. Because of the amusement this caused among adults not completely familiar with the depth of deprivation that existed in our family, I was prone to burst into song at the slightest encouragement and bask in the attention that followed. It was perhaps this attraction to the music of the masses that years later caused equal surprise and merriment when my pre-school son entertained the unwary on trains and buses with *She Was Only a Bird in a Gilded Cage* neatly demonstrating that he had the same desire to draw attention to himself as his mother at a similar age.

Just as our experience of music differed substantially from that of the generation that followed us, so did our experience of words. We may not have been educated to a level that might ordinarily be described as equipping us with an elevated vocabulary but it is true to say that there was a depth and richness to the language we were familiar with. Although by the 1960s and 70s daily life in North Kent had gone through enormous changes, three decades earlier it was not particularly unusual for the smallest child to ingest and assimilate ideas and knowledge unconsciously and so large tracts of verse were learned seemingly by osmosis and no-one considered this to be unusual. By the time local children were five years old they not only knew the words of the songs their parents and grandparents routinely sang, but also an assortment of prayers and a wide range of rhymes and jingles. The more determinedly religious had also absorbed and could quote a variety of Bible verses. The very first nursery rhyme I could repeat on command was when I was eighteen months old – *Hark, hark the dogs do bark, the beggars are coming to town, some in rags and some in tags and one in a velvet gown.* Six months later my repertoire had grown to include such ditties as *Bye Baby Bunting, Ride a Cock Horse to Banbury Cross, Lucy Locket Lost Her Pocket,* and *Goosey, Goosey Gander.* By two and a half I knew all routine nursery rhymes including a reasonably full rendition of *Who Killed Cock Robin.* This was not surprising because even those women lacking a substantial depth of maternal instinct and with a weakness for alcohol such as my grandmother, were somehow or other familiar enough with the oral tradition of England to be in a position to pass it on to their own children, who did similarly. And so those of my generation inherited a spoken folklore and became totally aware of nonsense jingles, lullabies, counting formulas, puzzles and riddles, rhyming alphabets, tongue twisters, nursery prayers and singing games. Under the circumstances it was not all that surprising that a selection of more impudent music hall melodies, though less suitable for infant consumption, were effortlessly added. We ended up holding a significant lexicon albeit quite different from that which might be familiar to those of a similar age today. Today's children burst into middle childhood with a remarkable amount of technical knowledge and are more than capable of making purposeful decisions regarding the operation of their mobile phones and iPads. Yesterday's children were privy to sizeable tracts of information that has largely disappeared and when we look back to examine it there even seems to exist a lack of purpose about it.

Every child of the 1940s and 50s was aware of the day on which they were born and the implications that was likely to have on their life. *Monday's child was fair of face* and Molly from number 31 had been born on a Monday. It was one of the reasons she was confident of becoming a Hollywood film star because she knew that she would grow up to have the looks for it. She said she would have been tempted to go into hairdressing if it hadn't been for her day of birth.

Joan Bennett was not so fortunate, being welcomed into the world on a Tuesday by her grandmother who announced at once her delight because *Tuesday's child was full of grace.* None of us understood all that well what Grace entailed but it was definitely important to her grandmother who had used it as a given name for Joan's mother back in 1909 even though she'd been born on a Wednesday. Years later the husband of Joan's recently married teenage sister who was Irish and found Joan difficult to like was heard to say she was graceless.

We were glad not to have to grow up as Mrs Ribbens' latest baby, Sonja-Kim – a *Wednesday's Child* and already *full of woe* judging by the amount of noise she could make which her mother said was just the Colic and something she would grow out of. Aunt Mag thanked the Lord that none of her four ever had the Colic.

My brother was considered a fortunate newborn because *Thursday's child had far to go* and Old Nan said he would do well in life just like her Edgar did when he managed to give up the drink. It was odd that she should have made this comment at all as she never managed to give up the drink herself. After a more than shaky start involving problems with the local law enforcement authority Bernard did indeed go far and accomplished much more in his life than any of us would ever have thought possible.

Friday's child was loving and giving and that description wholly suited the only Friday's child I knew, my cousin Little Violet who was unfortunate enough to have to live with our Grandmother but bore the difficulty admirably well even at Christmas when the crayons and colouring in book that had been promised her were not at the bottom of her bed on the morning of the 25th. She no longer believed in Father Christmas anyway she said and fully understood that the problem was because Old Nan had been too preoccupied with gin from The Jolly Farmers the day before to head down to Woolworths. Anyhow Little Violet told us that she wasn't that fussed about colouring in books and crayons because they were not always all they were cracked up to be and never worth the money. Next year, she decided, she was going to buy her own Christmas present. In the meantime she continued to be kind to everyone else and looked fearful and guilty when Uncle George seemed outraged when it became clear she was the only child in the family without a gift that year. He told the awkward collective of Constant sisters that he thought their mother was a disgrace. To make up for being overlooked he gave Little Violet two half-crown pieces and Uncle Harold not to be surpassed in generosity did likewise. She was of course quite delighted with the sudden improvement in her fortunes and later said it had been the best Christmas ever.

The oldest of my nearly grown-up male cousins, Young Harold who I disliked and distrusted, was fond of telling us that he would always have to work bloody hard because of being born on a Saturday and we all knew that *Saturday's child works hard for a living.* He had just got his first job down at Vickers and had recently bought a smart pair of tight black jeans and boots with heels and managed to attract his very first girlfriend so he felt superior and wanted to be treated as if he was twenty rather than sixteen.

By the time I was two years old I knew perfectly well that I was a very special child indeed having been born on a Sunday. We were all completely aware that *The child that is born on the Sabbath day is happy and wise and bonny and gay.* Even my grandmother was grudgingly appreciative of the fact that there was a lot to be said for being as fortunate as I was concerning the day of my birth though she insisted it had more to do with basic good luck than anything else. This was rather spoiled later, when at the impressionable age of fourteen, I was told that because my time of birth was midday it meant I was of a very shallow disposition as all the planets were above the horizon. I was forever destined to have only superficial ideas and a slight understanding of life and all my relationships with people would be at a surface level. I had no idea whatsoever what this would mean for my future but I immediately began to feel rather more shallow than was healthy. I knew my mother was still proud of my Sunday status even though she used to look at me sometimes and shake her head saying nobody would ever think I was a Sunday's child. She didn't really mean it and I felt it would not be fair to explain to her how shallow I was.

It would be accurate to say that back then more people were expected to know songs and hymns than are these days where the custom seems to have remained only in the villages of Wales. In the 1940s when women sang on factory assembly lines whether they were regarded as having good singing voices or not there was less self-consciousness as far as performing was concerned. My mother had a very good voice, inherited no doubt from my grandmother and when she sang people listened and complimented her. And so she became in the habit of doing so regularly and her singing formed part of my very first memories so frequently did I wake up to *Sonny Boy, Always, It Had To Be You, April Showers, After You've Gone, As Time Goes By* and *Night and Day*. So with complete ease the lyrics of popular song were also absorbed into my sub-conscious so that they too became part of my words and music frame of reference.

And faithfully The Wireless continued to ensure that we became acquainted with all the numbers that rose to the top of the popularity polls so that *Peg O My Heart* and *Now Is The Hour* became then remained firm favourites with me and my friend Molly before she went on to diversify and become Doris Day's No 1 fan, in the process becoming word perfect in yet another raft of lyrics. Not surprising perhaps, because this was still at a time when children could reliably sing the National Anthem and were familiar with the hymns loved by The Anglican Church. *Abide With Me, Rock of Ages,*

Jerusalem, He Who Would Valiant Be, also became so ingrained in memory that I would be able to recall them decades later during more intermittent Church visits. Undoubtedly there was something valuable to be gained from contact with our Christian mythology by way of occasional Church attendance with our school class because most of us, underprivileged though we were, and whether we came from a rock solid or decidedly shaky Christian background, came to have a firm knowledge of edifying moral tales. This provided us with a basis on which to judge our own behaviour and that of others whether we chose to do Right or Wrong. By contrast today's child would only barely comprehend righteousness and would have only a hazy idea of what might be meant by the words of the Twenty Third Psalm. My own family was one wherein the members indulged in a great deal of behaviour that was decidedly Wrong but at least I was completely aware of this fact.

It's tempting to believe that the working class children of our particular corner of North Kent were possessed of an undoubted educational edge over those that followed us, an edge that displayed itself in an ability to harvest language and use it productively and to react to the many and varied dimensions of music. And it is sobering to realise that if this is so it emerged from a combination of diverse influences. The unquestionably bawdy lyrics of the Music Hall together with the poetry of the King James Bible. The catchy melodies of Musical Theatre and the undeniably stirring strains of Anglican hymns. And for me the added sprinkling of operatic arias and Chopin waltzes that reliably reduced me to tears, courtesy of Roy Plomley.

A Remarkable Lack of Resilience

Growing up with very little was in many ways fortunate. You could even say that the troubled time in which we wartime children were conceived had in itself been providential and paved the way for the resilience that accompanied it because we were a remarkably robust bunch. For example, at a most basic level it was accepted that only girls cried. Boys did a sterling job of controlling the urge to do so even under extreme circumstances. By the time boys were five years old most of them were in total control of such displays of emotion and tears were reserved for the home, witnessed primarily by mothers and siblings because crying in the presence of fathers did not earn a boy much kudos. The only boy I knew who was known to weep on a regular basis was Colin Bardoe and he was frequently reduced to tears if a game did not proceed to his liking. His twin, Alan, was not given to the same weakness but then Alan was a different sort of boy altogether.

On the other hand, many girls, and I was one of them, were prone to tears at the slightest provocation. This did not mean that we were inclined to a general weakness of spirit, however, because overall we were just as emotionally sturdy as our brothers. Possibly this was simply what was expected of us in order that we should be able to cope with the ups and downs of daily life, the first of which may well have been starting school. Few under-fives were able to adjust to the idea of starting school by cutting their teeth at supervised playgroups. There was no such thing as visiting a local classroom prior to the day we were due to start, for a gentle introduction. Usually we were simply thrust into the education experience without much warning and expected to acclimatize. After a great deal of hysteria from many of us, acclimatize we did. Savage though it may appear to today's parents, such expectation did at least begin the process of preparing us for the fact that life was likely to throw some nasty surprises our way. The future would undoubtedly involve setbacks infinitely worse than being plonked unceremoniously within a strange room, alongside a dozen or more other wailing five year olds safely in the charge of a responsible adult called The Teacher.

By the end of our first school year we had learned that some of us had a reasonable aptitude for education and others did not. Those who mastered the first Readers with ease and learned to write in sentences with capital letters and full stops placed correctly were told we were Clever. Pressure was placed upon those unfortunates who could not Keep Up and a few children stayed in the Infants' Class for another year so by the time we were six years old we knew they were not Clever and often were even described as Slow. This was the fate of poor Alan Spooner who spent a great deal of time pretending to be a steam train in his second year of school in 1946. The unfortunate terminology that surrounded academic progress has long been abandoned of course and even by the 1960s the Clever children had become Antelopes and the Slow ones Tortoises. In 1973 my oldest son emerged from his first few months at a school in Auckland and proudly announced that he was a Bear and all the children who could not read the first Janet and John book were Monkeys. He was very glad not to be in the latter category and despite his tender years fully understood the implications.

At St Botolph's in the late 1940s quite a lot of playground bullying took place, particularly between groups of boys, and those exposed to it were expected to find coping strategies without resorting to the involvement of adults. Fights between boys took place on a daily basis and winners were lauded whilst the teaching staff appeared not to notice the level of barbarity. It was definitely a time of Winners and Losers and it would have been unthinkable to institute games where this was not the norm. When *Alice In Wonderland* was read to us in 1949 by our greatly loved class teacher Will Clarke, we all laughed heartily when the Dodo, after thinking long and hard about a race, decided, 'Everyone has won and all must have prizes.' Yet this is precisely what happened at a sports day in a local school in the late 1980s and I, to my chagrin, felt forced to issue participation certificates, if not prizes, to all attendees at my school holiday courses by the year 2000 in order that no child should feel emotionally sidelined.

It is a fact that children all over the world have become vastly less hardy over the years and today's seven-year -olds would find themselves quite unable to cope with the daily difficulties that plagued the lives of those of we who grew up in an earlier era. We in our turn saw our setbacks simply as part of Life because all around us the adults in both their conversation and attitudes made us mindful of the fact that there were other children who had greater problems and obstacles to contend with. The ten-year-old boy called Isaac with the odd way of speaking who had somehow or other lost his parents in a camp in Poland and was now visiting the most far-flung members of his family, was one of them. Though watchful the boy was not slow to make friends, join in games and seemed not to be in need of therapy. He and others like him went on to lead successful lives and showed little evidence of character weakness. Even our own parents and grandparents whose early lives we knew to have been much harder than our own grew to adulthood possessed of an inner strength and a great deal of fortitude.

Each decade that followed us has seen an inevitable progression of helplessness and vulnerability that has resulted in the astonishingly weak and dependent young adults we see around us today. These are the assemblies of youth who find themselves quite unable to cope with criticism, who see insults everywhere and are therefore affronted on a daily basis, who accuse all and sundry of racism, of sexism and any other ism you could possibly conjure up and who reach out for support at the slightest stumbling block. Counselling is required for moderate trauma, and in depth therapy for the kind of sexual assault we of an earlier generation might have regarded as a clumsy compliment. This lack of mental stamina has led to the inability of those under the age of fifty to take responsibility for their own life decisions and when things go wrong for them and there is no immediate and obvious prop there follows a feeling of growing panic. Often then, because the blame has to be apportioned somewhere, they lay it upon the shoulders of their ageing parents who somehow or other in the past made serious errors of parenting and failed to provide adequate emotional sustenance. This results in inescapable family rifts where grandparents are punished by being forbidden to see their grandchildren and perplexed seventy-year-olds are told that they have ruined lives with sins such as circumcision, vaccination, or the failure to observe talent that would have turned their middle aged offspring into stars of stage and screen.

It would be tempting to decide categorically that these frequently melting snowflakes are completely responsible for the lack of backbone they display but of course life is never that simple. What our generation is in fact responsible for is pandering to the inadequacies of the next generation, contributing to what made them weak and helpless in the face of the slightest adversity. It is a fact that the children who cannot deal with games featuring losers are likely to become the adults who dissolve at any hint of misfortune. They fail to handle the most minor of life's impediments, can only see rampant racism and sexism in cartoon drawings and fail to understand the humour. They must be protected from the dangers of Freedom of Speech for fear that speech might expose them to dangerous concepts and somehow or other their sense of judgement regarding relationships with the opposite sex has been irrevocably tarnished by their fear of being taken advantage of sexually.

On the other hand, we who had the good fortune to grow up in an earlier age, did not have to face the alarming myriad of choices that so beset those growing up today. Most of us were confident in the gender we were assigned at birth and the disturbing thought that we might select an alternative did not cross our consciousness. By the time we were eleven years old we were completely aware of our abilities, academic or otherwise, and knew that if we were Clever we might pass the eleven plus examination and if we were Average we were unlikely to do so and if we featured among the Slow children we would be afforded the safety and comfort of the D Stream. There was little room for confusion and no Suzuki Music Schools to lead us to believe that we might become concert violinists. Our parents were most unlikely to lead us to believe that we were good at something if we were not because by the time we reached school age we were expected to cope with the idea that talent was capricious. Along the way we came to the conclusion that moments of happiness could be sporadic and life was not always fair. And so little by little we were able to separate good luck from bad, sense from nonsense and truth from fiction. Sadly, somehow or other a great many of us have failed spectacularly to pass the simplicity of these notions on to our children and their resulting lack of resilience is quite remarkable.

The Shipping Forecast

Every classroom at St Botolph's School, with the exception of that which in those days we called The Infants' Room, devoted one entire wall to a map of the world. The British Isles was situated near the top on the left hand side and was mostly crimson in colour. Other areas on the wall map were also crimson and we knew this was because they were Ours, places that were part of The British Empire or loosely so, because the ownership was never explained completely adequately. Over time we learned quite a lot about these places and knew with some degree of accuracy where they were. Australia and New Zealand were Ours and had cities called Sydney, Melbourne, Auckland and Christchurch. There were a great many sheep there and forests that they called Bush where there were fires at certain times of the year because the temperature was much higher than in England. We were also familiar with far off Hong Kong because that also belonged to us even though it was somehow or other Chinese and China definitely didn't belong to us. We owned a great many places in Africa and they were also pleasingly crimson, as well as islands closer to home like Malta and further afield like Jamaica. Sometimes these countries became jumbled in our minds with others we had already somehow lost and those we were hoping to gain in the future. For reasons that never became entirely clear it was more important that we should be able to point out the whereabouts of Sydney or Hong Kong than cities like Liverpool and Edinburgh closer at hand. With this in mind we learned songs such as *Waltzing Matilda* and *Kookaburra Sits in the Old Gum Tree* and sang them with enthusiasm.

It was also of prime importance that we learned that we had always been a seafaring nation which is how we came to discover so many significant new lands and there wasn't much about the sea that we British did not know. We knew we were superb fishermen and our prowess in this area was legendary. The local shrimping industry meant that even before we started school we were all familiar with the Bawley boats on the Thames, the small coastal vessels peculiar to the estuary and occasional weekend trips also introduced the not to be overlooked Whitstable oyster boats. It was our greatly admired teacher Mr Will Clarke who was most instrumental in impressing upon us our relationship with the sea, and he who pointed out that our very own fishing areas were Thames, and Dover and possibly even Plymouth, and that if we took the time to listen in to the Shipping Forecast on the wireless we would learn about those further afield. It was produced by the Met Office he said, and broadcast four times daily. It had been suspended during the war years of course because we British had no desire to be helpful to Hitler and his U-boats by handing out too much information regarding conditions at sea. When I checked this out later with my mother it was to find that she agreed with Mr Clarke and said that there might well have been an invasion if the Shipping Forecast had remained and where would we all be now if that had happened? Speaking German no doubt! But of course she had always been strangely confident that the entire population would have taken to German effortlessly and on command. Fortunately for us, none of this eventuated and advice to shipping was happily reinstated in 1946 shortly after the ringing of church bells which she also welcomed.

Even my grandmother who had paid little attention to conditions on the high seas welcomed the return of the bells and to children of my age, having never heard them before, they had been a novel enigma. My cousin Margaret importantly informed me that had they sounded in wartime it would have meant only one thing – the dreaded Invasion. Then every village bell ringer would have hurried to sound them loud and clear to warn neighbouring settlements. She said nothing about the Shipping Forecast possibly because its return was to her not quite as dramatic. Nevertheless due to the influence of Mr Clarke its strangely hypnotic rhythm soon became as much a part of childhood to me as the reassuring radio chime of Big Ben, the only church bell I had ever known, sounding the hour at various times throughout the day.

Because I admired Mr Clarke so much and because the iconic Forecast was inherently hypnotic I became an avid listener though the geographical location of the oft repeated sea areas such as Viking, Forties and Dogger remained a mystery for decades. Faeroes, Hebrides, Cromarty and Malin only emerged with a reality that could be just half-imagined when my brother's interest in birds of prey took him to the furthest reaches of Northern Scotland. Nevertheless I carried on listening because after a year or two all listeners were destined to become devotees. Not that the habit improved my knowledge which even as a young adult remained decidedly sketchy.

Embarrassingly, I distinctly remember the excitement of applying for a job at a weather station on one of The Falkland Islands as a shorthand typist. I now feel certain that I had found the advertisement on the front page of *The Times*, at a time when that front page was still devoted to advertisements. Upon investigation I found that it was a place where I would find stunning beaches, an abundance of wildlife and a town called Stanley. Perhaps also a great deal of bad weather, at least that's what I was hoping for. How desperately I wanted that job, simply because I was certain it would take me somewhere between Faeroes and South East Iceland where undoubtedly I could feel an integral part of the Shipping Forecast for a year or two. A cautionary note sounded when I was told I would be entitled to paid annual leave in Argentina. Even I in my ignorance was completely aware that Argentina had never once featured in the much-loved broadcasts over the years of my addiction. Extricating myself from the two year contract that I had been so keen to sign only minutes beforehand was awkward.

Although the broadcast was definitely made several times daily I only reliably remember it late at night although what I was doing awake around midnight at the age of nine and ten is anybody's guess. Nevertheless for years the Shipping Forecast was essential to me, surpassing even *ITMA* and *Much Binding in the Marsh* and definitely knocking any children's programming out of the running. I showed little interest in Malcolm Savile's *Gay Dolphin Adventure* which was serialized shortly after the war and followed enthusiastically by my older cousins but somehow or other what was in store for fishing fleets became information I was unable to do without. I can distinctly recall giving a little shiver of delight as the soporific mantra began to intone ...... *Viking, Forties, Cromarty, Forth, Tyne, Dogger*...... and I once again slipped into the curious late night ritual that preceded sleep.

Although I was aware that the words and phrases were linked to the seas that surrounded our island invariably my mind would begin to sleepily explore the connected landscape, scanning the coastline and examining the water's edge as the North Kent marshland linked with the darkly ominous estuary. Then onward with courage into the more mysterious depths of the North Sea, spoken of at school by our beloved teacher in his introduction to the history of our country when he assured us how courageously we had resisted the advances of Viking and Norman invasion. What harm could possibly come to us nestling within our sceptred isle whilst violent forecasts for *Fisher, German Bight, Humber* and *Thames* impeded the progress of all would-be marauders? It would be a hardy plunderer indeed who would consider breaching the darkly churning waters of *Dover, Wight,* and *Portland.*

Invariably as the three-minute bulletin drew to a close, somehow I would have fallen asleep, safely tucked up in my bed and knowing very little of the perils involved in venturing out to sea. And possibly this ignorance can be forgiven as the only vessels I was entirely familiar with were still the Gravesend Bawleys that had the good sense to fish only for shrimps and largely avoid bad weather. Things might have been different had we lived in Hastings or Dover where perhaps the weather mattered more.

Regardless of how much the weather did or didn't matter, however, clearly the iconic broadcasts had a huge impact on me as they did on countless others and it was with some surprise and much pleasure when many years later I heard it featured on Desert Island Discs. More recently I have come to realise that it is much admired by certain poets such as Sean Street with his *Shipping Forecast Donegal*. One of my Auckland neighbours, hailing originally from The Midlands, is absolutely certain she heard a portion of it on an old late night episode of a re-run of *Prime Suspect* only a month or two ago. People of some note are even said to mention it in diary entries.

Despite years of firm fan-dom it has always been challenging to accept the terms used and what the jargon might actually mean. The weather terms are almost an argot no matter how patiently the Beaufort Scale is explained. Ordinary groups of words take on a meaning that sounds perverse such as *rain later – good. Veering north-westerly five or six, decreasing four. Rain then showers moderate.* I now know that wind direction generally is given first followed by strength on the Beaufort scale then precipitation followed by visibility. Wind direction is indicated by *veering* which simply means clockwise or *backing* – anti-clockwise. Strong winds above force 8 are described as *Severe Gale 9, Storm 10, Violent Storm 11 and Hurricane 12.* Visibility is described as *good* which means you can see about five nautical miles, *moderate* where you can see between two and five nautical miles and *poor* where you can see very little. Lastly when you can see nothing at all the conditions are described as *fog*.

This information ensures that it all becomes clearer and substantially less mysterious but then of course it is not always necessary to understand the language or even the reasons behind it, much like not needing to have complete comprehension of the Mass in Latin. Nor is it necessary to examine why after all these years, the forecasts are still broadcast at all let alone four times daily in a time when even the most modest vessel could be presumed to have adequate technology on board to provide the safety net needed. Perhaps mariners like the rest of us simply have a need to hear the mantra, to be assured that all is well with the world, to feel safe.

Broadcasting Carried On

For years we had an old copy of the Radio Times at our house, issued on 4th September 1939, price two pence which we pronounced 'tuppence'. The cover featured an impressive photograph of Broadcasting House in Portland Place under which was the assurance that Broadcasting Carried On! A banner of text was superimposed across the building proclaiming that this particular edition contained the Revised Programmes for September 4th to $10^{th.}$ Some dramatic changes in programming had clearly taken place due to the emerging conflict. The Home Service had been somewhat abruptly created and a great many of the BBC staff had been evacuated, not that my mother was really aware of that of course. She only rarely purchased the weekly magazine but on this occasion must have decided that we needed to be fully informed of what the future might hold for us and most especially for me, newly procreated and to be born the following year. The only print connection with the air waves that I was regularly aware of as I grew up was my older cousins' copy of Radio Fun which they fought over then usually passed on to us, supposedly for me but my mother devoured it eagerly. It featured Big Hearted Arthur and Dicky Murdoch on the front cover and Vic Oliver within its pages. These people became almost real to me and as I am sure I have said previously, I knew that they lived inside the wireless in a strange parallel world.

The Wireless itself was still relatively new and innovative in 1939, the year my parents were married in Crayford. My mother had been an early and enthusiastic listener on account of her brother Edgar actually building a Crystal Set in the 1920s which had elevated him to intellectual brilliance in the eyes of his numerous admiring sisters. Although the BBC had been launched as a private company as long ago as 1922 it had rapidly burgeoned in popularity and became a national corporation in 1926. By the first few months of 1938 more than six million receiving licenses had been issued and by the autumn of that year, shortly after the Munich Crisis, the British Broadcasting Corporation solemnly began preparations for what it saw as the inevitability of war. It was only natural that the company should see themselves as significant, even vital in the business of the struggles in Europe and those VIPs in government obviously felt similarly including Neville Chamberlain himself who was heard to say that the broadcasting of pure entertainment must surely cease once war began. This would have been devastating as far as my mother was concerned but oblivious to the feelings of minions like her he had already decided that the airwaves should be a vehicle for government advice and instruction together with hourly news bulletins. In order that the corporation be most effective and to avoid the possibility of information dissemination being disrupted by bombing campaigns, both National and Regional Programming were to be combined into a single channel called The Home Service which would broadcast throughout the country. Programming would still be produced in several different places to limit damage if one area was knocked out due to enemy activity. In fact Broadcasting House in Portland Place was to be hit twice but the BBC was never forced off air which they must have found gratifying at least in retrospect. Replacement provision had been made in Bristol from a disused funicular tunnel in Clifton gorge with the BBC Symphony Orchestra and Sir Adrian Boult in mind but when the Music Department moved to Bedford, Bristol became the BBC nerve centre in the West of England eventually sending programmes in more than thirty languages all over the world. None of the Constant sisters were in the slightest bit interested in the kind of music Sir Adrian Boult might concern himself with but they mourned the temporary loss of dance bands and they were certainly more than a little on edge about what might happen next if the war actually came to pass.

Early on the morning of 1st September 1939 Poland was invaded and it was this defining act of aggression that finally pushed Britain into decision and the BBC found itself all at once on a most serious footing which meant that the much mooted merging of the channels took place at once and was announced to listeners on the midday news. My mother, standing at the shallow stone scullery sink in York Road, felt a dull and ominous thud in her chest. It was a Friday and the fish for my moderately devout father's midday dinner was already simmering in milk with a sprinkling of parsley, the potatoes bubbling alongside. Although she was always to be an indifferent cook she could manage boiled fish in what she described as Parsley Sauce though sadly she never learned how to thicken the sauce.

When war was finally declared it startled those unfortunate broadcasters sitting in lonely, soon-to-be-abandoned studios, playing tracks from LPs and every ten minutes informing a dwindling group of listeners that their particular channel was now defunct. More than likely they like everyone else had confidently expected that the Start of War would herald an extraordinary bombing attack that would maim if not kill Britons in huge numbers. That did not of course happen. In fact nothing happened immediately and the housewives of Northfleet began to breathe easily again.

No official announcement was issued to the nation by Neville Chamberlain until the deadline for German troop withdrawal ran out on 3rd September. Hitler had perhaps wisely ignored those who expected a dramatic turnabout from him. In Northfleet my mother, her new pregnancy already suspected and undoubtedly half lamented, stayed close by the trusty wireless and wondered not for the first time about the prudence of the soon to be most unhappy marriage she had entered into. Bernard Joseph Hendy might well be a regular Mass attender, might never be heard to use bad language, might indeed not be a drinker BUT when all was said and done he was not her Fred. Fred her beloved fiancé was now five years in his grave, a victim of the greatly dreaded TB. It is fair to say my father had a number of pleasing attributes but in our house he was destined not to be loved.

She was not alone in her concentration on the wireless that day because most of the neighbours and indeed all our relatives in Crayford were equally attentive, and all were eventually rewarded with the iconic broadcast announcement that most of us have since become familiar with, after which the national anthem was played followed by a lot of information about how to conduct yourself during an air raid and reminders to be sure to carry your gas mask with you if you ventured outside. All this certainly promoted a feeling of unease in the community, particularly the focus upon gas masks. The protection device distributed to mothers for infants under three months was in the form of an alarming box operated via a foot pump. My mother had paid great attention to that issued to Totty Freeman from No 31 for her new baby registered and christened Edith but swiftly renamed Molly, and was consumed with anxiety as to what might become of the vulnerable infant should the mother herself succumb to poison gas or indeed prove not to be particularly adept at pumping. She was to be more than relieved the following year when I reached the required age to be allocated the more acceptable diver's helmet style mask that did not rely on maternal proficiency.

During these disquieting early days whilst mothers of the next generation anguished over what might lie ahead, the BBC came up trumps with regular tips on how to ensure the safety of the young and the only fault that could be found with the deluge of data was that the women delivering it were definitely of the Posh variety and most likely would not have any real worries themselves, at least not of the kind that preoccupied those living in the working class terraces of the South of England. Aunt Maud maintained you had to overlook the fact that they were undeniably more than middle class because there were times when you needed people like them, women who knew what was what. Anyhow they couldn't help sounding posh if they belonged to the Women's Institute because everybody knew you couldn't join unless you were at least a little bit posh.

Old Nan said that they were all looking up their own arses and you didn't have to take their advice if you didn't want to. My mother, on the other hand, always felt compelled to take the advice of those higher in status than herself and continued to feel doubtful. Interspersing the broadcasts were news bulletins and live music from Sandy MacPherson and his organ which everybody enjoyed even though he turned out to be a Canadian and not Scottish after all. Not that there was anything intrinsically bad about being Canadian of course.

So the British listening public continued to wait with bated breath for the onslaught of bombs from German aircraft and as the hours passed began to gradually relax when nothing untoward took place. By 6th September the BBC's Variety Department took a deep breath themselves and broadcast the first live revue of the war – *Songs from the Shows*, from their new headquarters in Bristol. Within a week *Children's Hour* had returned also and a week later *Band Wagon* was back complete with Arthur Askey at the helm. This was swiftly followed by *ITMA* which was hugely popular and had first started some months earlier. All the aunts were reassured, even delighted and Old Nan quickly decided that Chamberlain had got it wrong about the war in the first place although she was sure he'd done his best, adding generously that it couldn't be easy doing his job.

The Wireless went from strength to strength during those early war years, and by 1943 the Variety Centre had abandoned Bristol and was back in London but holding onto an audience with only one channel would have been far from simple. There was a compelling necessity for Popular broadcasting and at the time this meant music and comedy. *ITMA* remained undoubtedly the most popular wartime show. It starred Tommy Handley and Jack Train who posed as a range of characters including a German spy called Funf who in particular caused my grandmother great merriment. Each generated their own catchphrase such as 'I don't mind if I do', 'This is Funf speaking' and of course the iconic 'Shall I do you now Sir?'. The people of York Road were regularly convulsed with laughter at the antics of The Minister of Aggravation and those in The Office of Twerps. Old Nan became eventually more addicted to the first new hit show of the war, *Garrison Theatre*, which featured the kind of revues that had entertained the troops of WW1. The slightly boisterous and disorderly audience definitely appealed to her.

The Bassants next door quickly became fans of *Any Questions*, which later became known as *The Brains Trust* and was described as a general knowledge programme, serious in intention but light in character. Five experts discussed questions from members of the forces concerning such unlikely topics as philosophy, science and art. It became a huge success, attracting a regular audience of millions. The BBC Repertory Company produced half a dozen plays each week and these promised to appeal to the Average Listener although my mother had her doubts about this assertion saying that in her experience plays could not always be relied upon and that films were better all round, even though you had to go out and catch a bus and on Saturday nights even queue up.

Children were definitely well catered for as time went on. MPs like Megan Lloyd George gave educational talks about how Parliament functioned and there were also talks on World Affairs. Infinitely more popular though was serialized drama which included *The Water Babies, Ivanhoe, Little Women* and *Nicholas Nickleby*. In October 1939, Princess Elizabeth made her first broadcast on *Children's Hour* with a special message to Evacuated Children which later included messages from parents to those children who had been sent to North America, South Africa, Australia and New Zealand. This was of course most exciting not just to those directly involved but also those listening Ordinary people, not all of them posh, people with ordinary accents heard on the wireless! My aunts, however, maintained that those who had their children sent Overseas were not ordinary at all and could only be described as Nobs. Not everybody agreed with them.

By the end of 1940, when the Blitz was well under way and The Battle of Britain had come and gone, the population had adjusted reasonably well to the various onslaughts. London had become the seat of Governments in Exile for Norway, Belgium, Holland, Poland, Czechoslovakia, Yugoslavia and Greece and acted also as the headquarters of General de Gaulle. The services of the BBC were used to address people in all these countries with Holland having a regular slot called *Radio Orange* with Queen Wilhelmina giving the first broadcast. In January 1941 during the broadcasting slot allotted to the Belgians, it was suggested that the letter V for Victory should be used to symbolize resistance in Europe and within a few weeks the idea was gaining traction in occupied countries. By the middle of the year the letter V in Morse code became the signature tune of the programme and adopted the opening bars of Beethoven's *Fifth Symphony*. The French, always thought to have a high opinion of themselves, became particularly adept at setting anti-Nazi words to traditional folk songs and in occupied France the tunes were whistled enthusiastically. It would be true to say that families like ours were remarkably insular and never over fond of foreigners of any description, not just the more actively despised Germans.

Meanwhile the Germans were busily broadcasting an English language News Programme with the aid of Lord Haw Haw, actually of course, William Joyce. He most definitely became a wartime radio star and millions tuned in to hear him, resulting in every British child of listening age becoming completely familiar with him and how he should be Strung Up, or Hung, Drawn & Quartered. I am not clear if we entirely understood why he was so universally reviled but to make an enquiry of this nature would have only resulted in further diatribes concerning the fate that must surely await him so generally we did not probe too deeply. However, over time even the youngest of us became comfortably acquainted with the names of those regular broadcasters of the years 1940 and 1945. This was unsurprising since these people were regular visitors into our homes day and night so that they were almost akin to family friends, in much the same way as that list of social media Friends infiltrate the outer reaches of our lives today. Not Real Friends in the sense by which we normally understand the term but nevertheless shadow people we begin to consider we know well. By 1945 the list included Alvar Liddell, Freddy Grisewood, Wilfred Pickles, Elsie and

Doris Waters, and Joyce Grenfell amongst others. My mother would have wanted to include Vera Lynn who with her regular fifteen minute singing spot kept the nation's spirits up. And being a definite fan of vigorous piano playing for a time she would have very much wanted to add Charlie Kunz to the catalogue. By 1944, however, he had been abruptly tossed aside when a neighbour convinced her that Kunz was a close confidante of Goebbels, a definite German spy and thus sending messages to the enemy via the keyboard. This was on account of him having a German sounding name although later it appeared that he was more American than German but having lived in England for years definitely considered himself part of the British community. When he died in 1958 he was buried in Streatham Vale cemetery in London but Nellie Constant remained suspicious.

The part played by wartime broadcasting during the first half of the 1940s cannot be overvalued and radio fans like myself find it cheering that the technology, now more than a hundred years old, is still going strong, still invaluable during times of tension and trauma such as those created by recent earthquakes in Japan, Taiwan and New Zealand. Broadcasting has indeed carried on!

In Sickness & In Health

There has never been any doubt whatsoever that when it comes to death, the Irish do it better than most. My grandmother, although not particularly attached to the country of her forebears, having minimal allegiance to the Riordens and not especially bound to the Catholic Church, would generally come into her own on the occasion of a death in the family. She had an uplifting attitude to the conventions of a community. I clearly recall her determinedly putting out teacups on All Souls' Day for the two aunts recently taken by tuberculosis, each one leaving a newborn girl. One of my older cousins said it was in the hope of the dead returning but in his opinion that was a load of baloney and it would make life difficult if they did. This was because the one who still had a husband had just left him and both aunts had been sharing bedroom space in the ever more crowded house at the bottom of Iron Mill Lane. But he said all this softly and with hesitation fearing the clip around the ear it would earn him should he be overheard.

Despite their at times half-hearted attitude to the One True Church my mother's family was far too intimidated by the thought of everlasting fire to completely ignore the rituals expected of them. Wakes were essential and held a day or two before a funeral Mass, usually at night. The women cried a lot into their white handkerchiefs newly ironed for the occasion and the men talked about how wonderful the deceased had been and then everyone got drunk and ignored the children who fell asleep under the nearest table. These affairs, looking back on them, were inclined to be more elaborate when the newly deceased were male. As we were a family overburdened with women the more emotionally charged gatherings were few. After the Mass there would be a get-together at The Jolly Farmers where everyone got drunk once again. Occasionally there might even be a Memorial Mass a month or so later but there was no expectation of it.

My father, always a more committed churchgoer than my mother, might well have been seduced into the family in the first place by all the apparent devotion to the religion he had been raised within. Sadly, in the case of his own death few of the possible traditions were observed. Nobody would have thought to put out a teacup for him at the next All Souls' Day and the Wake, if indeed there was one, would have been a subdued affair. This might have been simply because my mother was theoretically making all the necessary decisions and she had always harboured a certain amount of hostility towards the Church and in recent years a great deal towards her husband. Decades later my brother's demise occasioned a similar disregard, for similar reasons. No matter how elaborate the memorial event held some months later might have been, the stylish venue, the champagne and smoked salmon canapes could never erase the indifference to what basic Catholicism demanded and what he would have expected had he been able to voice an opinion. The imperilling of his immortal soul by dispensing with such traditions was glaringly obvious to all family members, lapsed though they might be, if not to his cheerfully atheistic wife and her relatives, creating little pools of discomfort here and there. My cousin Margaret courageously observed that she had now outlived two Bernards and added that neither death had elicited the Send Off she would have expected. Then she fell into silence when her daughter, my second cousin Jane-Marie, who once upon a time was simply called Jayne, pierced her confidence with the kind of gaze intended to do exactly that. But a moment or two later her mother added in a voice both daring and tremulous that our grandmother would never have allowed such a thing to happen and Jayne, stuck to her mother like glue for reasons best known to herself, looked confused because she had little direct knowledge of her notorious great-grandmother who had died when she was still an infant.

It would be true to say that Old Nan was totally prepared to throw herself into all that was customary and went hand in hand with a relative's passing, and perhaps this was not entirely because the end of life was also associated with a great deal of alcohol. She was always the first to busy herself with the covering of mirrors and ensuring that all photographs were laid face down. This was because she was in every respect a superstitious woman and when we walked with her at night she was at times apt to insist that we walked in the middle of the road so as not to disturb the spirits of the wayside even when that wayside consisted merely of the meagre little front gardens of Iron Mill Lane. She once told me that the stubs of funeral candles could be beneficial when laid on burns. She warned us all to take care when walking in graveyards and not stumble close to new graves for to do so would ensure we would be dead within a year and so of course we walked very carefully indeed.

Generally she avoided the marshland so loved by my teenage cousins Harold and Leslie with their rabbiting rifles when they set off down the creek. The Crayford Marshes directly flanked the early estate housing and lay beyond The Jolly Farmers and The London Road, and it promised all manner of exciting activities but our grandmother asserted that it was the Ruin of the lungs and hers in particular. The Hearts of Oak roll ups she determinedly smoked, she assured us helped to counteract the deadly vapours that rose up from the damp terrain and delivered Marsh Fever. She was strangely unconcerned about the layers of cement dust that coated the roofs of Stone Village, a few miles further down the river and passed regularly on the 480 bus route to Gravesend. There was something slightly exotic about the riverside village of Stone that had grown so rapidly during the middle of the nineteenth century, sprouting row after row of Victorian terraced housing to accommodate the local cement factory workers. When I was six or seven years old I was convinced that the grey-white covering on rooftops and bushes was a kind of everlasting snow, unyielding to the heat of summer, and I had envied my cousin Little Doris, whose mother had died at her birth simply because she and her father Poor Arthur Steele had briefly lived there. My Grandmother would gaze fondly from the windows of the bus and comment that years ago she had spent many a happy hour with her Edgar at The Brown Bear that lay just beyond the Alms Houses and that she had pitied the women forced to live in Them Places, crowded in together and never once allowed an evening out at The Bear even though it was right there on their doorstep.

Even at the time I marvelled at the fact that she and my father viewed the area quite differently, he telling me a great deal about the local castle that was made completely of flint and built as long ago as the reign of King Stephen, whenever that might have been. Neither of them seemed unduly concerned about the effects of the cement snow upon the health of those living in the area.

In comparison, Northfleet and its surrounding environs seemed then a surprisingly healthy place in which to live considering the amount of industry that polluted Thames-side settlements at that time. If you avoided renting those houses closest to the various cement works, you were unlikely to be overly bothered by the contamination they caused though conversely neither would you be so close to your probable place of employment. All this meant you simply had an important choice to make and any repercussions would be nobody's fault but your own.

At that time one of the most common causes of death was Tuberculosis known as Consumption and it penetrated local families with a quiet persistence determinedly stealing away youthful health and vigour. My mother said she had wept copiously when Greta Garbo died in a film called *Camille* in 1938, shedding far more tears than had fallen for Phyllis, her younger sister. Phyllis had been the extrovert, always happy, always sharing a joke and yet she had succumbed so readily to the illness becoming pale and thin and dying within a year.

By the time I was a pre-schooler and more aunts had perished, my mother had developed an exaggerated fear of Consumption despite the fact that there was by then an assurance that medical treatments were rapidly improving and very soon a cure might be possible. This fear was handed on to me to whom she elaborated upon the state of the sufferers among our immediate neighbours. These information updates ensured that I hurried past their homes and dared not breathe until I had safely passed the places where the not-yet-deceased but dangerously disease-ridden victims lived. When Mrs Morris, whose bouts of coughing could be heard from dawn to dusk, decided to donate the remaining bones of each Sunday dinner to our decidedly underfed pet dog, I risked being savaged by regularly wrestling them from his jaws once she had safely disappeared back through her scullery door, for fear he would contract the disease. And if he happened to win the occasional struggle, for the next ten days I hovered around him ever vigilant that he might start coughing in a dry and tubercular manner. Fortunately he did not but the weekly combat changed our hitherto friendly relationship and he found it hard to forgive me which he demonstrated by treating me to menacing looks coupled with an occasional snarl and refusing ever again to join me for walks around St Botolph's Churchyard.

Although the condition did not seem to easily affect canines it continued to spread with ease from person to person. Sometimes the newly afflicted were sent to special hospitals called Sanitoriums where they remained for months at a time, enjoying gentle walks in the fresh air and good, wholesome food. One of my uncles even sent his two daughters to Switzerland, the place where Heidi and Peter spent their time tending goats but then he was said to be Flash and Made of Money. Many sufferers were thus destined to recover but there was a strange reluctance among a proportion of the working classes to actually avail themselves of the opportunity of such a cure.

Patsy Pitt, who lived in Springhead Road and was therefore almost but not quite middle class decided she would take the offered Cure. This was not simply because of being almost middle class but also because she had at the age of thirty found herself a Young Man called Alfred to whom she quickly became engaged only weeks before finding out that her sudden weight loss was the first sign of the illness. Concerned to ensure she would be fit for her planned summer wedding she agreed to three months on the South Downs without argument as long as her beloved would agree to visit every Sunday without fail, which he did. She was later devastated to find herself jilted shortly after finding herself cured and sank into a deep depression. My mother said she did not have much sympathy since Alfred had kept his word about the visits and had waited until she was pronounced well before casting her aside for an usherette who worked at The Majestic. In her opinion Patsy Pitt should simply Get On With It as she herself had been forced to do when her Poor Fred had perished in similar circumstances back in 1930. Whenever Poor Fred was mentioned, which was never ever in the presence of my father, she paused a moment, eyes glistening, and might then perhaps be forced to brush a tear from her cheek because no matter how hard she tried she had never been quite able to stop loving him.

There would be no exaggeration in saying that in the middle of the twentieth century the health matters that most troubled our community differed vastly from those causing anxiety today. Children in particular were more at risk back then and unlike today, parents more eager to take advantage of any government schemes such as mass vaccination that would protect them. There was no need for medical personnel to explain that vaccination was a miracle of modern medicine and that it would save more lives worldwide than any other medical product or procedure. Uneducated though we were there existed a tacit understanding that this was so and in those days there was no knowledge of afflictions such as Autism and those stumbling across it would have been unlikely to recognize it as something that was undesirable or that could have been avoided. They would have found any assertion that it might be connected with their child's recent vaccination very hard to believe. There was an acceptance that in the midst of any group of children there were those who were different, slower than the norm, with visual or hearing defects, or suffering from an inability to control their impulses. The latter were seen as wayward, described as badly behaved and might be beaten more than was customary and if their parents failed to sufficiently quell their behaviour with violence at home, regular canings could be doled out at school that often had the desired effect.

So we were all vaccinated against Smallpox when we were under two years of age and apparently many children had an unpleasant reaction to the inoculation with high temperatures and were perhaps sick and fretful for several days. Some of them might well have gone on to develop conditions now associated with the vaccine but unlike today the attendant gossip about such matters did not particularly proliferate around the neighbourhood. There were no radio Talk Back Programmes on which to air concerns, no television and nobody knew what Support Groups might be. What most pre-occupied our parents was that we should not fall victim to the truly terrible illness that had killed and maimed so many of their own generation. The vaccine did not come accompanied by doubts and uncertainties.

Old Aunt Maudie who lived at the top of York Road was profusely pock-marked and in her eighties and her opinion was that Smallpox was a malady that struck with guile and without pity and should never be under-estimated. She was not anyone's real aunt and her neighbours had quite forgotten whose aunt she had originally been except that his name was Humphrey. He had not even been a proper nephew but the son of one of her cousins from Southend who had died in the Flu epidemic just after the Great War. She said the Smallpox when it settled upon her family in the latter part of the nineteenth century seemed to be just a cold in the head and nothing more than that. Victoria was still Queen, it being just before she also adopted the title Empress of India, the very same summer in which the Chapel organized an outing by train to Ramsgate. They had lived in Chatham at the time on account of her father's work in the Ropery at the dockyard. Both she and her older sister Gracie had been chosen to go on the outing because of their good behaviour and oh how they had enjoyed themselves. What tales they had to tell when they returned. Gracie had even won a prize at Hoop La –

a set of wooden alphabet blocks which she intended to give to their youngest brother who was about to reach his fourth birthday. It was to be a surprise and she hid the box under the bed she shared with Gracie in the attic. None of them were accustomed to birthday presents.

Then they both began to feel unwell and as the days passed her mother had never known such girls for crying and complaining just for the sake of runny eyes and noses. It was surely giving her The Pip and so they tried as hard as they could not to make The Pip any worse. Then she and Gracie began to vomit and to feel much worse. It had taken more than a week for the tell-tale blisters to make their appearance and my goodness didn't they cause a deal of dread and trouble. At first they seemed perhaps harmless, just little pink clusters but she and Gracie knew it must be bad from the extent of the fear and fright on their mother's face. They wondered how long it would be before they recovered. Maudie remembered it was more than two weeks before the scabs fell off and it was then she first became aware that at some stage during that terrible time her sister had died and had even been buried for there was no longer any sign of her. Nobody in the bed beside her, no longer a sister to squabble with or to share secrets with. She remembered the alphabet bricks and checked that they were still hidden which they were.

She, Maudie, had been lucky really and most especially when you considered the fact that despite her poor mother's best efforts The Smallpox had not been content to take just Gracie and within weeks the three little brothers aged six and five and very nearly four were similarly seized, two of them passing in one night.

The youngest never did reach his milestone birthday and so never knew about the wooden blocks won by his big sister which was a pity really. And now all these years later Old Maudie couldn't for the life of her remember what happened to them. She did remember though that her poor mother had never really recovered from that time of The Smallpox and the loss of four of her five children. And in recent years Dr Crawford had told her that it was a good thing her mother had once been a milkmaid but what he meant by that was not clear except it was something to do with all the children dying.

My father when regaled with the story upon his return from the six to two shift said that several boys admitted to the Chatham Orphanage he grew up in were there because Smallpox had killed so many in their families. And because he thought it was interesting he added that what was more the disease had been active in Egypt thousands of years before and those that dug up mummies had found evidence of it. My mother said she found that very hard to believe and qualified this remark by explaining that she meant the bit about Egypt, not the orphanage. He replied that the scourge of Smallpox would probably be with us for all time, vaccinations or not. But he turned out to be wrong about that of course. It's hard now to know what Old Maudie would have thought about the fact that Smallpox was destined to become eradicated from the face of the earth within two decades.

In the 1940s and 1950s a range of childhood illnesses that are becoming far less familiar to us today such as Measles, Mumps, Rubella and Scarlet Fever, were run of the mill and every child was expected to encounter them at some stage, suffer the effects that would hopefully be temporary and emerge all the stronger for the experience. There were after all, far more critical onslaughts on the child body. There was Polio for example that nobody wanted to contemplate although oddly enough it had a habit of largely ignoring the working classes and concentrated on those more affluent, the toffs from the smart houses on the London Road, and even those from more moderate homes in Springhead Road. Why this should be was not clear and when a vaccine appeared it was received with relief and delight because everyone in communities like ours had at least heard of children whose lives had been devastated by the disease even though the death rate seemed to be lower than other more feared illnesses. In the late 1940s Polio had spread throughout North Kent. Swimming pools, cinemas and schools closed and the fear of its direct visitation became visceral. There were tales that the more badly afflicted became unable to breathe and lived their lives inside something called an iron lung whilst others recovered with only a limp to show for it. For some children months had to be spent in hospital. I was rushed to the local doctor one morning by my alarmed mother simply because overnight I had developed a stiff and painful neck. And in the waiting room other parents pulled their children just a little further away from me and left the chairs on either side of us empty. Dr Outred examined me carefully, taking twice as long as was customary for him and with tight lips and narrowed eyes so that I became slightly alarmed myself, turning over in my mind everything I had heard about those unfortunates who fell into the clutches of

Poliomyelitis. But I was to be reprieved and in our immediate area only Joyce Martin of Dover Road fell victim to it, was hospitalized for seven months and left with a pronounced limp.

The greatest fear of all was reserved for Diphtheria known as Dip, the sore throat that killed and was passed effortlessly from child to child. In 1942 three and a half thousand British children died from the condition compared with what have been a mere four deaths in the past twenty years which fact should do just a little to indicate the positive aspects of vaccination. In 1946 Grace Bennett's Joan developed a Bad Throat with attitude, and became so ill that her mother feared she had somehow stumbled across the infection and took a torch to peer into her throat, imagining she could clearly see a grey membrane. Old Mrs Bassant next door, whose adopted daughter Ina had been a victim years previously, but luckily survived, was called upon to give her opinion which she did and it was to call the doctor even though it was seven in the evening and a Sunday. This advice was coloured by the fact that in 1923 young Ina had all but perished and had been taken hurriedly to the Gravesend Sanatorium in Whitehill Lane where there were beds for those with infectious diseases. She had been lucky in more ways than one because only a few years before she would have had to be taken to Strood where it cost eight shillings a day and the medical care was not all that it might have been. Gravesend that year had a total of sixty beds of which sixteen were allotted for Diphtheria, twenty for Scarlet Fever and twenty four for Smallpox and the cost of care was three guineas a week. When Ina was there first class care was given by a Matron and two proper nurses with the help of a couple of trainees. It was well worth the exorbitant fee for those who could afford it. They had been stretched to afford it but their Ina was well worth the financial sacrifice. The Matron had said that left another day she might well have had to have a tracheotomy which was where a hole is cut into the throat in order to ensure the patient can breathe. It just didn't bear thinking about and Grace Bennett should get the doctor to her Joan as fast as possible.

When he finally arrived that evening, charging five shillings and sixpence and slightly ill-tempered because he had been intending to spend the entire evening sorting his boyhood stamp collection into the order he had long imagined would increase its worth, he said it was not in fact The Dip at all. Their Joan was suffering from a common or garden Quinsy. Apparently a Quinsy was a tonsillar abscess and although in some cases it could be serious in this case it was, in his opinion, not as Joan's Quinsy was now with his help, to be adequately treated. Her mother was left wondering if she would have been better advised to leave consulting him for his advice until the following morning when the cost would have halved because this was in the time before the National Health Initiative. Most people thought better safe than sorry and even today Diphtheria kills up to ten per cent of sufferers but because of widespread vaccination programmes is now rare in the developed world.

When the National Health Service was finally introduced and news spread throughout the working class streets of Northfleet that consulting a doctor with a sick child would no longer cost half a crown there was disbelief from some. My mother said she had never begrudged the money in the first place, which was not completely true. My grandmother wondered if the free visit would actually result in the kind of care that was worth having in the first place. But within a short space of time the community was reassured and free health care together with the development of vaccination programmes had the intended result.

Over time there were to be fewer funeral processions where the youngest child mourners dressed in white and less mournful burials involving little white coffins. Mr Horlock and his sons were to be asked less frequently about the possibility of a white plumed horse-drawn hearse even though Old Aunt Maudie said it had always been a sight to behold and that the streets of Chatham had been wet with tears the day her little brothers were buried.

My grandmother, who would have been the first to note that as time went on white plumed horses became an option reserved for The Toffs, said that back then all hearses were pulled by horses anyway and white plumes were commonplace. She recalled that when their little Arthur was taken, her Edgar had Polly the little Shetland pony decked out with the finest equine headdress he could find and she was made to pull a goat cart with the little white casket on it all the way from Maxim Road to Dartford cemetery. People had stopped in the streets and men removed their hats and the women all cried. I didn't ask what childhood malady had snuffed out the life of Little Arthur but I wondered. A long time later my brother, having done a great deal of family history research, told me that more than likely the infant Arthur had been smothered accidentally in the bed of his parents who in those days drank far more than was good for them or their children. So many aspects of the lives of children have changed for the better.

The Coming of the Postcodes

To my knowledge our corner of North Kent was postcode-less during all the time it took me to grow old enough to triumphantly leave at last and make my way up-river to London. My very first encounter with postal codes was when I moved importantly into the bed-sitter lands of South Kensington and Bayswater conscious of being very grown up indeed. To me these strangely disconnected and incomprehensible letters and numbers were simply part of the mood and character of a city I had longed to be a part of and added to the thrill of at last living there. London postal areas were established as long ago as the 1850s and the system was gradually adopted by other major cities, the process considered to be completed by 1934. It wasn't until 1959 that the then Postmaster General first trialled the plan throughout England starting with Norwich and apparently a gradual nationwide rollout followed and was at last concluded in 1974.

At some stage during those years Gravesend and Northfleet received their very own postal codes with DA12 bestowed upon Gravesend East, including Chalk, Shorne and Cobham and the now familiar DA11 awarded to Gravesend West which included Northfleet. It's perhaps surprising that the Thameside community that had grown so rapidly during the nineteenth century had to wait so long to be elevated into the ranks of a Place with a Postcode. It would not be an exaggeration to say that the area had been a centre of industry for centuries with the Romans giving commerce a kick start when they first began to dig chalk from the area. Cement-making followed without too much delay and by 1796 one James Parker, a former clergyman, had set up kilns on Northfleet creek in order to make what he called Roman Cement. The cement industry went from strength to strength with nine plants eventually operating along the riverside, providing a great deal of employment for the locals, one of whom was my father. It had taken some time for Bernard Joseph Hendy to shake off the glamour of foreign travel that the war had afforded him and for several years he regularly reduced both my mother and myself to boredom with his tales of the sunshine, dates and olives of North Africa and the music and food of Italy. Often these reminiscences ended in tears for my mother who would later mutter to her sisters that he didn't say much about the Fancy Women with the foreign names and that there was no mistake that the war had definitely been the Ruin of him.

To be fair he didn't always talk about life in far-away places and how superior it had been to that he was now forced to live and after a few months back in North Kent he seemed to develop a keen interest in the social and industrial history of the area. It was he who told me that there had once been a number of dockyards in Northfleet that had over time produced many impressive vessels. One, laid out in the late 1700s, was owned by a shipwright called Thomas Pitcher. A list of ships he built included at least two dozen for the East and West Indies services along with many a vessel for the Navy. Pitcher's yard finally closed in 1860 and more recently I have learned that a local group of enthusiasts as fascinated as my father had been in the late 1940s are now involved in investigations to reveal more about it. Sadly back in the time when my well-meaning father sought to interest me in the topic I couldn't have been less attentive to details of Mr Pitcher's shipyard.

Information concerning the nearby paper industry possibly would have absorbed me more because I loved to draw pictures and as I got older to write stories and I was destined to grow up one of the few extremely fortunate children provided with a seemingly limitless amount of suitable paper at a time when it was in very short supply. The paper industry had sprung up during the first decades of the twentieth century in the form of Bowaters then Bowater Scott where my Uncle Walter reigned supreme for many years as a foreman and eventually a union representative. He clearly also had a habit of methodically helping himself to a wide variety of paper products which he concealed in a sack on the back of his bike and delivered to our house at least once a week on his way home to Waterdales. I don't know how many of his own large family of children were similarly supplied although his youngest daughter Connie always seemed to be able to locate paper on which to draw patterns for dolls' clothes, but I was able to create endless towns, villages, flower gardens, intricate maps of imaginary islands, short stories and plays for stage and radio, etc, year after year. It has only recently occurred to me that this purloining of paper was in fact a very serious matter, particularly so at a time when it was a most valuable commodity. Clearly these thefts were never brought to the attention of anyone in a position of seniority at Bowaters because Uncle Walter seemed to go from strength to strength on the factory floor.

The cable works originally called Henleys and later AEI were yet another noteworthy employer and occupied part of the former infamous Rosherville Gardens. It is proudly claimed that the PLUTO pipeline (PipeLines Under The Ocean) invaluable during WW2, was built there. Uncle Walter's daughter Connie chose them as her first employer when she left Wombwell Hall School, and became an office girl for Henleys. This was a definite affront to her formidable father who had specifically directed that she should do the Domestic Course at Wombwell Hall in order that she learn to cook and sew for her future family. He was alarmed at the thought of her joining the ranks of more modern thinking schoolgirls like myself who had chosen to take up shorthand and typing and were in danger of having their heads turned as a result. At sixteen years of age Connie's head had finally turned and she struck out for independence and began to take evening classes in typing and talk loudly about her father's views being stuck in the Dark Ages. This was in some measure due to the influence of her first boyfriend, Mick the apprentice builder, who had definite plans for their future together and was unafraid of her dictatorial father.

None of us knew a great deal about the one time notorious Gardens at Rosherville that had been the brain child of George Jones and certainly proved a splendid use for the motley and dispirited group of abandoned chalk pits. Although from time to time Old Nan made mention of what a Grand Day Out it had been to go by steamboat to Rosherville and that at Easter time the hats had to be seen to be believed and what a black day it was when the gates closed for ever. They had apparently been one of the largest and most popular of the Victorian pleasure gardens and survived from the accession of Queen Victoria for more than seventy years into the reign of George V. At the time there were a number of extensive pleasure gardens in the London area including Vauxhall near Lambeth on the south bank of the Thames and Cremorne on the river at Chelsea. Smaller gardens also proliferated such as those in Marylebone and Islington both of which had been frequented by Samuel Pepys as long ago as the mid1660s. On one occasion Pepys had gone to Islington in great excitement to drink China Tea only to complain bitterly later about the price of the rather indifferent roast chicken he was forced to order for his hungry female companions. And more than two and a half centuries later my young grandparents, as yet unburdened by the many children they were later to have and celebrating a win at the races, made a very similar complaint regarding the cost of the boiled chicken available at Rosherville. Old Nan maintained that she reckoned it was Daylight Bleeding Robbery and no mistake and in any case the remodelling of the Bijou Theatre into a modern refreshment room had been a gross blunder on the part of the organisers and only served to increase the already exorbitant prices. Except she didn't actually put it like that.

Although the gardens in the chalk pits declined in popularity over time, for a glorious epoch they towered above similar possibilities for entertainment in the marshy region that sat alongside the Thames and was ultimately to become part of a future postal code. The sectioning of that corner of North Kent into easily distinguishable alphanumeric cyphers would take place long after the little Greek temples and statuary in the cliffs, the archery lawn, the bear pit, the maze, the visit of the American Sousa band and the performance of the great Blondin, Trapeze Artist Extraordinaire had been completely forgotten.

Jeremiah Rosher and his son Joseph who had given their names to the building scheme that saw the advent of a clutch of smart new houses appearing in the area in1830 were great enthusiasts of the Gardens and would undoubtedly have approved of their estate eventually becoming absorbed into the coding system that was to develop many years later. It was evident even as the freshly drawn plans for Rosherville New Town were presented and displayed to all in the neighbourhood who might be interested that the pair had great hopes for the development. Their first prospectus states confidently that it was predicted the area would become to Gravesend what St Leonards and Broadstairs had already become to Hastings and Margate. For a time the homes attracted at least a percentage of those the Roshers had envisaged but over time they would slowly but surely plummet in popularity and by August 1939, when my newly-wed parents inspected a top floor flat in Burch Road, the rot had definitely set in. The road had been named in honour of Jeremiah's father-in-law Benjamin Burch and a hundred years previously had been the smartest place in the district to live. On the eve of WW2 it was what my mother termed a Pig Sty, a slum with no laid on water and a lavatory shared by all and sundry in the house and as the front door seemed permanently open, no doubt by half the street as well. Having been born in a hop garden and brought up variously under tarpaulins in fields and condemned Victorian terraces, her assessment was significant. The fact that the famous Rosherville Hotel still stood nearby in all its architectural glory did nothing to alter her opinion. My grandmother said she remembered the hotel in its Glory Days when it was full of mirrors and plush settees and red velvet drapes but added that it had been a hospital during The Great War and in her opinion it was them wounded troops that ruined the place.

During the next war, impatiently waiting to begin, German aircraft were to fly regularly through the Kentish skies above DA11 and according to the residents of York Road, Northfleet where my parents eventually decided to take up the rental of number 28, would deal the worst blows to daily life experienced for centuries. For a time it seemed little might remain of the age-old Thameside communities, little left to be sectioned into alphanumeric districts at the behest of some future Postmaster General.

On the other hand misfortune and catastrophe ebbs and flows and good sense dictates that any situation on a busy waterway would always offer an obvious place for a potential phoenix to arise from hypothetical ashes. The river would of necessity provide a reliable water supply and the means for transporting raw materials and products. The local woodland might at all times be called upon to offer the timber needed for industrious endeavour. And amid the ever-abundant supply of chalk was also flint that at various stages of community development would be found expedient as a building material.

That segment of DA11 now called Northfleet derives its name from its situation on the most Northern reach of Ebbsfleet once simply called the River Fleet. Few who pass through the international railway station of that name that emerged so rapidly a few years ago in Ebbsfleet Valley would know or care that in 600 AD the river was known as Fleote by the Saxons. Neither would they have much interest in the fact that by the time the Domesday Book was completed the little town was known as Norfluet or even that the settlement on the other end of the Fleet is called Southfleet and these days recorded as being in postcode DA13. There might be some transitory interest in the fact that the Bluewater Shopping Centre that I have so far never visited, lies nearby and that the station is part of the Thames Gateway Urban Regeneration, a project of national priority and that it is a mere hop, skip and a jump from the M25 motorway.

Flashing through Ebbsfleet aboard the Eurostar a few years ago I was astonished to catch a glimpse of St Botolph's Church standing proudly atop of the cliffs that border the long ago chalk excavations and fall as they always did, abruptly into bramble pits. And just for a moment, enduring memories of times past surfaced and demanded to be examined. Long ago summer evenings with my mother and Molly, our younger brothers lagging behind and complaining of hunger, thirst and tiredness, foraging for mushrooms among the brambles as the shadows grew longer. Sunday mornings with my grandmother at nearby Springhead, past the pig farm and the abandoned fever hospital, intent upon gathering the wild watercress that had first been cultivated there by Mr William Bradbery in the early 1800s for supply to London.

And because it was Sunday, being ever aware of the bells of St Botolph's loud and clear that must be ignored and those of Our Lady of the Assumption, more indistinct and muffled, but nevertheless to be heeded because they were calling us to Mass. If we had time we would go, we said one to another but knew that it was unlikely that we would do so. The gathering of watercress to go with shrimps and whelks for tea was infinitely more engrossing.

Other books by Jean Hendy-Harris

CHALK PITS AND CHERRY STONES
A Childhood in Kent

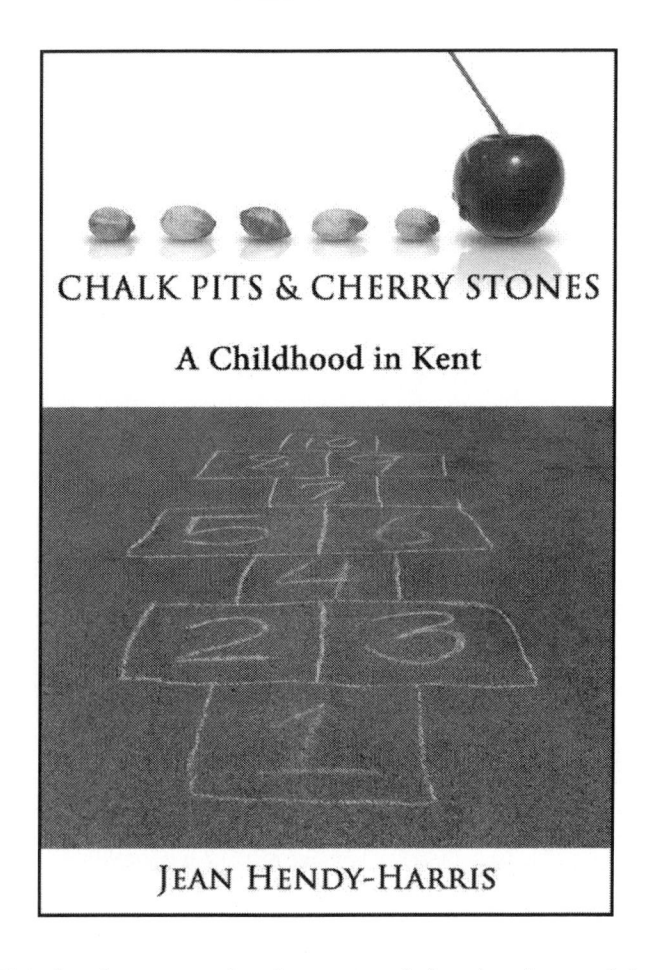

This book covers the dramas and deprivations of the author's earliest years.

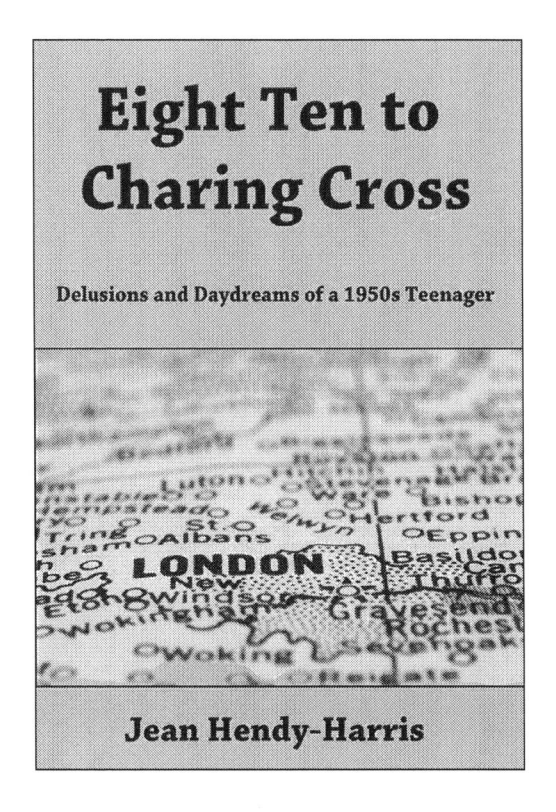

EIGHT TEN TO CHARING CROSS
Delusions and Daydreams of a 1950s Teenager

Eight Ten to Charing Cross

Delusions and Daydreams of a 1950s Teenager

Jean Hendy-Harris

In the second part of her memoir Jean continues her story as a teenager in the 1950s. Yearning to escape the confines of her working class family and a mundane future as an office worker via a fast track to fame and fortune, she settles for the reflected glory of typing for the rising stars of popular music. Meanwhile her rich fantasy life becomes ever more elaborate.

IN DISGRACE WITH FORTUNE
A Chronicle of Harlotry

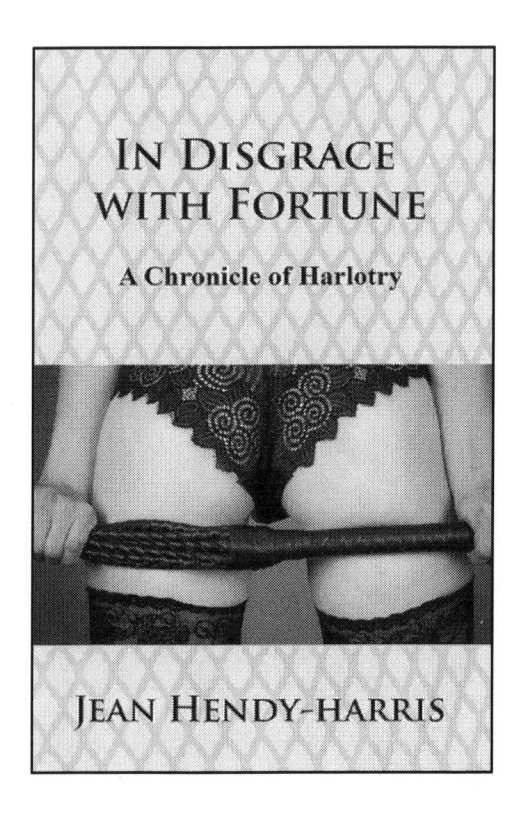

In this adult memoir Jean applies for a job as a showgirl at a London night club. Later, after a drama-filled affair, she applies for a job with a smart business in Belgravia catering to a wide range of 'unusual' clients. In her spare time she begins to write articles and short stories for magazines.

All Jean's books are available from Amazon in print and on Smashwords as ebooks.
Please consider posting a review to help other readers to enjoy the author's work.

Printed by Amazon Italia Logistica S.r.l.
Torrazza Piemonte (TO), Italy